DR. HEINERMAN'S
HEALTHY
HOMESTYLE
COOKING

JOHN HEINERMAN PH.D.

PRENTICE HALL
Paramus, New Jersey 07652

Library of Congress Cataloging-in-Publication Data

Heinerman, John.
   [Healthy homestyle cooking]
   Dr. Heinerman's Healthy homestyle cooking / John Heinerman.
     p. cm.
   Includes index.
   ISBN 0-13-761297-4 (paper)
   1. Diet therapy—Recipes.   I. Title.
   RM219.H45   1998
   641.5'63—dc21   97-36664
                                               CIP

Printed in the United States of America

10 9 8 7 6 5 4 3 2 1

ISBN 0-13-761297-4

ATTENTION: CORPORATIONS AND SCHOOLS

Prentice Hall books are available at quantity discounts with bulk purchase for educational, business, or sales promotional use. For information, please write to: Prentice Hall Special Sales, 240 Frisch Court, Paramus, New Jersey 07652. Please supply: title of book, ISBN, quantity, how the book will be used, date needed.

PRENTICE HALL
Paramus, NJ 07652

A Simon & Schuster Company

On the World Wide Web at http://www.phdirect.com

Prentice Hall International (UK) Limited, *London*
Prentice Hall of Australia Pty. Limited, *Sydney*
Prentice Hall Canada, Inc., *Toronto*
Prentice Hall Hispanoamericana, S.A., *Mexico*
Prentice Hall of India Private Limited, *New Delhi*
Prentice Hall of Japan, Inc., *Tokyo*
Simon & Schuster Asia Pte. Ltd., *Singapore*
Editora Prentice Hall do Brasil, Ltda., *Rio de Janeiro*

Warmly dedicated to
Orson Pratt and his brother Parley Parker Pratt
and Master Cook Dick Stucki

ACKNOWLEDGMENTS

The author gratefully acknowledges the generous assistance of Rose Write of the Home Economics Dept. of Vita-Mix Corporation; Certified Master Chef Walter Leible of Phoenix; Culinary expert and food critic Dick Stucki, editor of the *South Salt Sentinel* and columnist for *Utah Prime Times* monthly newspaper; my grandmother (father's side of the family) Barbara Leibhardt Heinerman (for some very old recipes); Annette Blue Elk of the Lakota Sioux (for several Native American dishes); food gourmet specialist Percival Winthrop of the *London Times*; food therapist Gisela Sawatzki of Salt Lake City; sous chef Michael O'Reilly of Dublin, Ireland; Stewart Ellis of The Whole Grain Co. (Toronto, Canada); nutritionist Gayle Sayers, Ph.D. of Boston; registered dietitian Heather Williamson of San Francisco; Liu Chen, owner of the Imperial Dynasty Restaurant in Taipei, Taiwan (for a few recipes); Rosie Sanchez, a curandera (folk healer) in Taos (for some Hispanic dishes); and Ron Seibold of Pines International in Lawrence, Kansas for fully converting me to the revitalizing benefits of field-grown wheat grass and barley grass.

INTRODUCTION

Many years ago, a general practitioner by the name of Henry G. Bieler, M.D. wrote a book appropriately titled, *Food is Your Best Medicine* (New York: Random House, 1966) which became an overnight bestseller. Briefly stated, the medical position he took was this: improper foods cause illness, but proper foods cure disease. His approach was quite unique for his time—food therapy rather than drugs was his favorite prescription for getting well and staying healthy.

I was twenty years old when I bought a copy and read it from cover to cover. Many of the health principles advocated within its pages served as a beacon of light to me as I marked out my own path in the great healing adventure of life. During his fifty years of medical practice, this California-based doctor treated film stars, coal miners, politicians, businessmen, farmers, blue-collar workers, and even some society dowagers. His numerous experiences with many of them served as wonderful inspiration to me in the books I began writing. Now, after a quarter-of-a-century and with more than fifty books to my credit, I can look back with great satisfaction in knowing I've been able to influence hundreds of thousands of people worldwide toward better health. These have ranged from peasants and politicians to physicians and priests.

Although my healing career began mostly with herbal medicine, it eventually acquired a much larger life of its own as I expanded more into folk medicine and the wonderful realm of food therapy. Finally, I came full circle to what Dr. Bieler had always advocated when I started writing my series of health encyclopedias for Prentice Hall Direct. That is, *everything* pertaining to health and wellness that I had been a diligent proponent of for so long, finally dove-tailed with Dr. Bieler's own curing philosophy and folded into what has become for me, simply *food therapy*.

I hope that you, the reader, will find a lot of good from the great variety of recipes contained within these pages. Not only are they flavorful and fulfilling, but also invigorating and energizing to your body's health. They are intended to not only make you well, but also to keep you that way for a very long time. They are relatively simple and easy to fix, but extremely nourishing. You will, indeed, derive better health from *my* style of down-home healthy cooking.

In the meantime, if you still have a problem, "take two radishes and call me in the morning," as I've been in the habit of telling people for many years now. You can reach me by phone at (801)-521-8824 or simply write to me: Dr. John Heinerman, P.O. Box 1471, Salt Lake City, UT 84147. You'll probably find me in the kitchen, rather than my research center, whipping up some more delicious *food therapy* meals for future health books.

Your friend,
John Heinerman
Fall 1997

CONTENTS

Contents

APPETIZERS

BROILED FRESH FIGS AND DATES

9 slices bacon

some Roquefort cheese

12 fresh figs

some cream cheese

12 unpitted dates

a few slices of ham

Cut bacon into pieces long enough to wrap one time around figs and dates. Remove hard stem end of figs and make a gash on sides with a sharp paring knife. Mix together equal quantities of Roquefort and cream cheeses and fill the figs; wrap in bacon, securing with wooden pick. Pit dates and fill with equal quantities of cream cheese and ham; wrap in bacon, too. Thread figs and dates on long skewer and broil, turning several times, until bacon is crisp. Serve hot from skewer or keep hot in small covered dish. (This recipe comes from Eileen Gaden's *Biblical Garden Cookery* with the kindness of the publisher.)

Serves 3–4.

I've served this dish on many occasions to rave reviews. Be sure to shop for the freshest figs possible.

FIG DELIGHTS

2 cups freshly-milled brown rice flour
1 1/2 cups freshly-ground sunflower seeds
1/2 cup tofu

1 1/2 cups dried figs
1 cup apple juice
1 tsp. ground cloves

Simmer figs in apple juice until they become soft. Then blend this fig-apple juice mixture in a food blender or push it through a wire sieve. The quantity should make 1 cup of fig puree. Combine this puree with the remaining ingredients.

Then add just enough water to form a stiff dough. If the dough is too sloppy, add some more rice flour. If it's too dry, add more liquid. The important thing here is to have a soft, moist dough that forms easily into a log shape.

Wrap wax paper around the log of dough and put it in freezer for 20 minutes or in refrigerator for 1 1/2 hours. It can even stay in there overnight, if necessary.

Preheat oven to 350°F. With a thin-bladed sharp knife, slice log into thin biscuits (about 1 1/4" thick) and lay them out on an ungreased stainless steel biscuit tray. Bake for 25-35 minutes. Try biscuits after 25 minutes to see if they are done; if required, bake longer.

Remove biscuits from tray to prevent further cooking. Cover them with towel while they cool. When cold, store biscuits in an airtight container.

Makes approximately 6 biscuits.

Hot, hot, hot—eat carefully, but feel the energy and vitality lift!

HORS D'OEUVRES FROM HELL

(for pastry dough):
1 1/2 cups flour
1/8 tsp. salt

1 4-oz. stick of butter (avoid margarine at all costs!)
1/3 cup goat's milk

Mix flour and salt together. Work butter into flour mixture. Add goat's milk and mix only until dough comes together and can be formed easily into a ball. Wrap in oiled wax paper and refrigerate 2 hours before rolling out.

Heavy whipping cream (that hasn't been whipped) can be substituted for goat's milk. This will at least reduce some of the heat; to maximize it, though, substitute grapefruit or pineapple juice for milk or cream.

(for hors d'oeuvres):
1 batch of dough
1 12-oz. jar of whole Habanero peppers
1 12-oz. jar of whole jalapeno peppers
1 8-oz. package regular cream cheese
1/2 cup nonfat yogurt

1 oz. fresh cashew nuts, finely chopped
1 oz. fresh pistachio nuts, finely chopped
1/4 tsp. sea salt
1/4 tsp. coarsely ground black pepper
1/4 cup ice water (approximate)
1/4 cup buttermilk (approximate)

Make pastry dough. Wear rubber gloves and work in a well-ventilated kitchen. (If you don't you will be sorry!) Pour off the vinegar in which the habaneros and jalapenos are packed and discard it. Rinse peppers well 3 or 4 times in water, remove and discard stems, but leave seed intact if the ultimate pain and misery is desired! Then set both kinds of peppers aside on a clean dish towel to dry.

Next mix cream cheese and yogurt together. Add both types of chopped nuts, salt and pepper and stir until well blended. Using your gloved fingers, stuff the habaneros and jalapenos with this mixture. Then roll the pastry dough out very thin, and use a Mason fruit jar lid to cut it into circles about 6" in diameter. Place one stuffed habanero and jalapeno apiece within each circle. Then with your gloved finger, apply a light coating of ice water to the edge of dough, neatly fold over, and seal. Prick an air hole or two in top of each tart with a toothpick.

Place tarts on greased cookie sheet and bake at 450°F. until crust is golden brown (this takes about 12–16 minutes). About 7 minutes before they are finished, brush top of each tart lightly with buttermilk; feed any remaining milk to neighborhood cats. Remove tarts from oven and permit to cool for 3 hours before daring to serve.

Makes about 4 dozen fiendishly delightful hors d'oeuvres which are better nibbled at by the timid and prudent, than wolfed down by the reckless and foolish. These tarts live up to their name and are quite "hot as hell"!

THE ULTIMATE GUACAMOLE DIP

4 large peeled, pitted ripe avocados
2 tbsp. minced fresh onion
1/8 tsp. cayenne (optional)
1/2 tsp. dried kelp
2 8-oz. cans peeled tomatoes, drained, or 1 large, fresh tomato, chopped

1/4 cup plain yogurt
1 tbsp. lemon juice
1/2 tsp. Worcestershire sauce

Mash all ingredients together in large bowl until well blended and smooth. Chill before serving. Use natural corn chips from local health food store for dipping.

Makes 3 cups.

The avocado tree grows in semi-tropical climates—Orchards are found anywhere from Santa Barbara, California to Lima, Peru. Today, Southern California harvests about 60 million avocados each year.

Delicious—anytime, anywhere.

MILD FLAVORED SALSA

2 large ripe tomatoes, diced

1 small onion, minced

6 cloves garlic, minced

2 green onions, sliced

4 small tomatillos or 2 large tomatoes, minced

3/4 cup cilantro, finely minced

In small bowl, mix all ingredients. Refrigerate for at least 1 hour to allow flavors to blend and juices to come out. Serve with your favorite tortilla chips. This is one salsa you'll definitely enjoy, because there are *no* chili peppers in it to bite you back!

Makes approximately 2 cups.

The herbs in this recipe lend a lively, refreshing taste. Try it!

WATERCRESS DIP

3 cups watercress, stems removed

1/2 cup small basil leaves

1 tbsp. liquid Kyolic garlic (available from any health food store)

2 tbsp. extra virgin olive oil

1/2 cup Parmesan cheese, grated

3/4 cup Pet evaporated milk (or an equivalent brand)

1/4 cup walnuts, finely ground

2 green onions, finely minced

granulated kelp for flavor

In a blender, combine watercress, basil, liquid Kyolic aged garlic extract, olive oil, and Parmesan cheese. Process until somewhat pasty. Then add milk and pulse only until mixed; be careful *not* to overmix. Transfer mixture to bowl and stir in walnuts and green onions. Add kelp for flavor. Dip will automatically thicken as it stands.

Makes 1 1/2 cups.

NOTE: The fat content of this dip is one-half that of standard commercial dips!

This was first served to me in a cafe in Doha, capital of the Arab kingdom of Qatar.

LIP-SMACKIN' APPETIZER

tahina (made from finely ground seeds of sesame)   *garlic*

dark red port wine   *lime juice*

dark rye bread

Mix tahina (usually available from Mideastern gourmet shops) with a little dark red port wine and flavor with finely minced garlic and a hint of lime juice. Mix well together into a paste and serve with chunks of dark rye bread.

Can be both a healthful appetizer or a dressing for any mealtime vegetable.

OLIVE BREAD SPREAD

1/2 lb. Calamata olives   *1/2 cup grapeseed oil*

3 garlic cloves   *kelp to taste*

Combine all ingredients in a food blender. Puree for 2 minutes. Makes 3/4 cup olive paste. Serve on bread or as meal appetizer.

CRANBERRY NACHOS

Surprising as this appetizer sounds, it is actually a delicious way to serve cranberries. The crisp nachos and creamy coulis and salsa make a hearty finger food.

Needed (for red and yellow pepper coulis, 1/2 cup each):

1 whole yellow bell pepper

1 whole red bell pepper

4 tbsp. extra light pure virgin olive oil

granulated kelp to taste

Needed (for nachos):

12 blue and gold tortilla chips

1/4 lb. chevre cheese (preferably a mild Californian or French variety)

radicchio

4 sprigs cilantro

Needed (for salsa, 1 cup):

1/2 cup cranberries (1/4 pint)

1/4 cup fresh orange juice

1/4 medium red onion, diced

1 fresh jalapeno pepper, diced

2 tbsp. chopped cilantro

1/4 cup fresh lime juice

pinch salt

freshly ground pepper to taste

sugar to taste

For red and yellow pepper coulis: Char whole peppers over an open flame or under preheated broiler. Place in metal bowl and cover tightly with plastic wrap. Let sit for 15 minutes. Then wash off all charred skin and puree in two batches (1 for each pepper) in a Vita-Mix whole food machine or equivalent food machine until smooth. Drizzle olive oil over each coulis batch and season with salt and pepper.

For salsa: Cook cranberries in orange juice for a couple of minutes, until tender. Place cranberry mixture in bowl and add onion, jalapeno, and cilantro. Toss with lime juice and add salt, pepper, and sugar.

For nachos: Preheat broiler. Arrange blue and gold chips on cookie sheet. To each chip, add 1 tsp. each of yellow and red pepper coulis and top with salsa and chevre, broken into pieces by hand. Put pan under broiler until chevre softens (about 5 minutes; it can get slightly browned). Remove from broiler. Arrange chips on serving plate. Form a bowl out of radicchio leaves and fill with extra salsa. Garnish with cilantro sprigs and serve immediately. Serves 4.

ROSE PETAL SANDWICHES

4 oz. light cream cheese or goat cheese

1/2 to 1 cup fresh rose petals

granulated kelp for flavor

8 thinly cut slices of seven-grain, whole wheat, honey wheat, pumpernickel, or dark rye bread (crust removed)

In small bowl, combine cheese with one-half of rose petals. Wrap well and refrigerate overnight. Spread cheese on 4 pieces of bread and press in the remaining rose petals. Place second piece of bread on top and cut into quarters diagonally. Serve with warm chamomile tea.

Makes 4 sandwiches.

SWEET POTATO CANDY

2 large sweet potatoes (about 1 lb.)

1 egg yolk, beaten (save whites)

2 ripe bananas

1 tsp. lemon juice

1 tbsp. allspice

1/2 cup ground walnuts

2 tbsp. grapeseed oil

Clean sweet potatoes (unpeeled) and boil until tender. Peel and mash with banana, egg yolk, lemon juice, and allspice. Refrigerate until thoroughly chilled and then form into balls. Refrigerate again for a half-hour. Roll in egg whites and nuts and lightly fry in grapeseed oil until golden brown.

Serves 4–6.

SOUPS

During my visit to the Soviet Union in 1979, I met an old gentleman in Leningrad whose father had been the personal chef of the last of the great Russian czars, Nicholas Romanov. Through an interpreter I learned a marvelous beet-cabbage soup (called borscht in Russian) that his father had prepared for the Romanovs.

PALACE BORSCHT

12 oz. roast duck (or chicken or turkey) carcass

2 (10 1/2 oz.) cans condensed beef broth plus 2 cans water _or_ 4 cups beef stock

1 1/4 cups chopped, peeled raw beets

3/4 cup sliced celery

3/4 cup sliced carrots

3/4 cup sliced green onions

2 tsp. grated ginger root

1/4 tsp. dried kelp

2 tsp. caraway seed

3/4 tsp. grated orange peel

1/2 tsp. dried basil leaves

1/2 tsp. dried thyme leaves

1/2 cup tomato puree

1 1/2 cups apple cider

1/4 cup vodka

1 cup shredded cabbage

1 tbsp. brown rice syrup

Place poultry carcass in 350° oven and brown for 1 hour. Bring beef stock to boil. Add poultry carcass. Reduce to low heat and simmer for one hour before straining. Return broth to pan. Add beets, celery, carrots, green onions, ginger, kelp, caraway seed, orange peel, basil, thyme, apple cider, vodka, and tomato puree. Stir together well; simmer for another 30 minutes. Add cabbage and brown rice syrup. Simmer another 15 minutes.

Serves about 6.

A vegetable delight!

MIRACLE CARROT SOUP

5 1/2 washed, unpeeled carrots
8 cups water
1/2 tsp. kelp
1/2 tsp. sea salt
1/2 tsp. honey

1/2 cup chopped onion
6 tbsp. melted butter
6 tbsp. flour
2 cups hot milk

Finely chop carrots. Combine them with water, kelp, sea salt and honey. Cook for 1 hour. Add chopped onions and simmer on low heat for 10 more minutes. Melt butter in skillet on medium to low heat. Slowly stir in flour, but don't brown. Simmer for 10 minutes without burning, stirring frequently. Then add hot milk to skillet and whip smooth by hand with wire whisk. Add this to soup, whipping thoroughly by hand until well mixed.

Serves 6 (or can be refrigerated and used for medicinal purposes whenever necessary).

A vegetable delight!

Asparagus was cultivated in ancient times by the Romans. The vegetable is a member of the lily family, and grows likes weeds on the seacoast of England and in the southern parts of the USSR and Poland, where the tundra steppes are literally covered like a carpet with this garden delicacy.

HOT ASPARAGUS-BROCCOLI-PEA SOUP

1/2 cup peas, frozen or fresh, steamed
1/2 cup broccoli, steamed
1/4 cup fresh asparagus, steamed or canned
1 tbsp. onion

1/2 tbsp. Kyolic liquid garlic extract
1/4 tsp. chicken bouillon or soup base
1/2 cup chicken broth, hot
1 tbsp. low-fat cheddar cheese

Place all ingredients in the order given in a blender. Secure the lid in place and run on high speed for 2 1/2 minutes until creamy smooth.

Makes 1 1/2 cups.

Fresh from the garden and sure to please!

CREAM OF CAULIFLOWER AND PEA SOUP

2 cups chopped cauliflower

3 cups shelled peas

8 cups water

1 cup sliced onion

1 tbsp. olive oil

1 whole bay leaf

1 tbsp. arrowroot flour

1 cup cold water

1/2 tsp. granulated kelp

4 cups liquid from boiling peas

more kelp to flavor

Chop up cauliflower. Shell fresh peas and set aside. Prepare water. Slice onion. Heat Chinese wok, add olive oil and chopped onion. Saute until onion is transparent. Add cauliflower and lightly saute. Add some water to cover vegetables and bay leaf. Cover and simmer 12 minutes. Remove bay leaf and blend soup until creamy. Add more water if necessary. Dissolve arrowroot in some cold water; add kelp to soup. Stir arrowroot into soup and bring it to rolling boil. Pour into individual bowls.

Next bring peas to rolling boil in 4 cups water. Cook 5 minutes. Blend in small amount of cooking water until creamy. Add rest of cooking water to measure 4 cups or until desired consistency is reached. Pour into saucepan and heat until boiling. Slowly pour into one side of serving bowl already containing cauliflower mixture. Using spoon, gently coax peas in.

Makes 4–6 servings.

Food historians believe kale to be the first form of cabbage to be cultivated. The Scots love it and so do I.

KALE AND SPUD SOUP

1 1/4 cups chopped medium onion

6 small Pontiac (red) potatoes, scrubbed and diced

9 medium kale leaves, chopped

2 1/4 cups water

1 tsp. basil

1 tsp. marjoram

1 tsp. rosemary

1 tsp. sage

1 tsp. thyme

1/4 tsp. finely chopped licorice herb root (Glycyrrhiza glabra), if available fresh or dried from any local health food store or herb shop

pinch of chili pepper for flavor

dash of granulated kelp for flavor

2 cups soymilk

Place onion, potatoes, kale, spices and water in a pressure cooker. Cook over high heat until pressure regulator starts bouncing around; then reduce heat to low and cook an additional 2 minutes. Remove pressure cooker from stove and let it cool on its own. Blend cooking mixture in a food processor along with remaining ingredients. This will have to be spaced out in several batches. Reheat and serve.

To make this soup without a pressure cooker, use a large, covered pot and follow instructions previously given. Simmer vegetables until kale is tender, or for about 35 minutes. Add more water if needed; soups cooked the conventional way require a lot more liquid than those made in pressure cookers.

Serves 4.

This soup is great for cold, wintery days! Mushrooms are among my favorite foods.

Naturopathic physicians in Europe, America, and Canada for years have recommended stinging nettle and saw palmetto together for whatever ails you.

GOOD CREAM O' MUSHROOM SOUP

1/4 lb. mushrooms

2 1/2 cups water

2 tbsp. butter

2 tbsp. whole wheat flour

1 tsp. salt or kelp

2 cups milk

parsley for garnish

Wash and skin mushrooms and simmer skins in 1/2 cup water. Mushroom caps and stems should be chopped into small pieces and 2 cups water added to skins. Simmering should continue until skins are tender.

Melt butter in another saucepan, adding flour and salt. Add milk gradually over low heat, stirring constantly with wire whip until mixture eventually thickens. Blend with cooked mushroom mixture. Then add chopped mushrooms and sprinkle with chopped parsley before serving.

Serves 2.

CREAM OF NETTLE SOUP

1 1/2 qts. nettle greens

1/3 cup Perrier or other mineral water

1/4 cup sesame seed oil

1/4 cup whole wheat flour

3 cups canned goat's milk

kelp, to taste

Cook nettles with water in covered saucepan over medium heat for 10 minutes. Cool 15 minutes, then puree in blender or food processor. In saucepan warm up oil and stir in flour, mixing well. Then slowly add goat's milk and cook until mixture thickens over a low heat. Add pureed nettles and heat thoroughly. Add some kelp to season.

Serves 4.

ONION AND GARLIC SOUP

Sensational after a day of skiing or a winter hike!

1/4 cup butter	1/2 tsp. crumbled thyme
6 large onions, peeled and finely chopped	4 cups chicken stock
4-6 large cloves of garlic, peeled and minced	4 large eggs
1 tsp. whole-wheat flour	1 cup Gruyere or Emmenthaler cheese, grated
2 cups dry white wine (Chablis)	1/2 cup whipping cream
sea salt and coarse kelp, to taste	

Heat butter in heavy flameproof casserole. Add onions and garlic and saute until onions are light golden brown. Stir in flour and saute for 2 minutes longer. Then add wine, sea salt, kelp, and thyme; simmer, uncovered, over low heat for half an hour, stirring from time to time.

Next add chicken stock, bring back to boiling point, cover and cook in preheated moderate oven, 350°F. for 2 hours.

Serve soup in four small ovenproof soup bowls. Beat eggs separately and add one to each serving, stirring it into soup to mix well. Sprinkle with Gruyere or Emmenthaler cheese and cook in oven for 10 minutes longer. Add 2 tbsp. whipping cream to each serving. Serve immediately.

Serves 4.

NOTE: If desired, the eggs and whipped cream may be omitted; just use cheese and return to oven briefly.

Legend has it that this hearty soup helps put off old age.

CREAMY ONION SOUP WITH FLOWERS

2 large onions, thinly sliced
1 tbsp. sage or thyme flower oil
2 1/2 cups nonfat milk
1 1/2 cups water

pinch of granulated kelp for flavor
5 tsp. whole wheat flour
5 tbsp. nonfat yogurt mixed with 1 tsp. lime juice
sprigs of parsley and flowers to garnish

In saucepan, sauté onions in oil on medium heat for 2 minutes. (If herb oil isn't readily available, then just use extra virgin olive oil instead.) Reduce heat to low, add milk, 1 cup water, and kelp. Cover and simmer for about 1/2 hour or until onion is tender.

In a small bowl, blend flour with remaining water, and stir into pan with onion mixture. Increase heat to medium high, bring to rapid boil and cook, stirring constantly, until slightly thickened. Remove from heat and add yogurt and lime juice. Reheat but without boiling this time. Serve garnished with parsley and flowers.

Serves 4.

Peas were Thomas Jefferson's favorite vegetable and who can argue with that learned gentleman's taste?

GARDEN PEA SOUP

1 tbsp. butter
1 cup diced potatoes
2 cups Perrier water
1 cup distilled water

1 cup freshly shelled green peas or frozen and thawed peas
1 tbsp. chopped chives
kelp to taste

Melt butter in a 2-qt. soup pot and swirl potatoes around in it. Add both kinds of water and simmer until potatoes are soft, about 20 minutes. Puree in blender and return soup to pot. Bring to boil and put in fresh green peas. Cook them until just tender—test by eating one—and stir in chives before serving. Season with kelp.

(This recipe adapted from *Eat Better, Live Better,* courtesy of *Reader's Digest.*)

SPANISH PURSLANE SOUP

Purslane is widely distributed from Greece to China. It's an excellent food for counterbalancing vitamin and mineral deficiencies.

1 cucumber, peeled and coarsely chopped

1 1/2 cups purslane, washed

2 medium tomatoes, peeled and coarsely chopped

1 medium onion, coarsely chopped

1 small green bell pepper, washed and coarsely chopped (leave seed pod intact)

1 large clove garlic, coarsely chopped

1 cup tomato and mixed vegetable juice

1/4 cup extra virgin olive oil

1/4 cup red wine vinegar

1/4 tsp. granulated kelp

for croutons:

6 tbsp. extra virgin olive oil

1 large clove garlic, finely chopped

1/4 tsp. oregano

1/4 tsp. basil

1/4 tsp. granulated kelp

6 cups French-style white bread cut into 1/2" cubes

In a food blender, puree cucumber, purslane, tomatoes, onion, green bell pepper, garlic, juice, olive oil, vinegar and kelp. This should probably be done in several batches so as to assure complete pureeing. Chill in refrigerator for at least 2 hours.

Shortly before eating soup make the croutons. In a 10" to 12" skillet over medium heat, warm the oil. Then add garlic, oregano, basil and kelp. Stir and add pieces of bread. Monitoring for any signs of burning, brown bread until crisp and golden, stirring frequently. Serve soup and croutons separately. This recipe is modified from the famous gazpacho served in restaurants in Madrid, Seville and other cities throughout Spain. It is absolutely delicious.

Serves 3–4.

Many American and English people don't fully appreciate salsify as other Europeans do. One can visit a number of fine restaurants in France, Belgium, Luxembourg, Austria, Switzerland, and Germany and find this herb served with various dishes. This is a delicious soup to improve your appetite.

SALSIFY CREAM SOUP

1 bunch of salsify, washed, scraped, and cut into small pieces

6 tbsp. butter

1 medium onion, finely minced

1 qt. white stock

6 tbsp. rice

pinches of salt, pepper and nutmeg to flavor

8 tbsp. unwhipped cream

2 well-beaten egg yolks

Briefly sauté onion in melted butter in medium pot before adding cut-up salsify root. Continue cooking over medium heat for about 6 minutes, stirring constantly. Then add white stock and rice. Cover with lid, turn heat to low, and allow to cook until rice is done and salsify root is tender. Strain liquid through a fine sieve, retaining the solids. Put solids into blender and puree thoroughly. Put puree back into same pot and add just enough of reserved stock to give mixture a smooth, creamy texture. (Don't add too much, however, or else you'll wind up with a soup of runny consistency.) Bring to rolling boil on stove, and sprinkle in the three seasonings. Reduce heat to low setting and add cream and eggs; stir briskly with wire whisk, but don't let soup boil again.

Serves 2–3.

SQUASH SOUP

1/4 cup virgin olive oil

4 medium onions, chopped

2 tsp. thyme leaves

1/2 tsp. ground nutmeg

1 lb. rutabagas, peeled and diced

2 lb. Pontiac potatoes, peeled and cubed

16 cups peeled, cubed banana, Hubbard, acorn or Golden Acorn squash, or pumpkin (7 lb.)

3 1/2 qts. fish stock (made from boiling fish heads, bones and fish scraps together)

Heat oil in 10-qt. pan over medium-high heat. Add onions, thyme, and nutmeg and cook, stirring frequently, until onions are soft (about 15 minutes). Next add rutabagas, potatoes, and squash; cook, stirring occasionally, until vegetables become tender (about 25 minutes). Then pour in fish broth and bring to boil over high heat; reduce heat, cover and simmer until squash mashes easily (about 1 1/4 hours).

Cream vegetables and broth, a little bit at a time, in a blender or food processor until smooth. If made ahead, let cool; then cover and refrigerate until next day.

Serves 10.

Squashes originated in the new world and were introduced to the conquistadors by Native Americans.

Pumpkin and squash make great soups. But from my own experience, squash makes the better version because it adds a depth of enhancing flavor that pumpkin can't quite seem to match.

CREAMY SQUASH SOUP

2 cups chopped, peeled potatoes

2 cups chopped, peeled acorn squash

1/2 cup chopped onion

1 1/2 tsp. snipped fresh marjoram (or 1/2 tsp. crushed, dried marjoram)

3/4 tsp. instant chicken bouillon granules

1 minced clove garlic

1/8 tsp. pepper

2 cups milk

cardamom

In a large saucepan combine spuds, squash, onion, marjoram, bouillon granules, garlic, 1 cup water and pepper. Bring to boiling. Reduce heat and simmer, covered, about 20 minutes or until vegetables are tender. Transfer about half of vegetable mixture to a blender container or food processor bowl. Cover and blend or process until smooth. Repeat with remaining vegetable mixture. Return all to saucepan. Stir in milk and heat through, but *do not* boil. Lightly season with dash of cardamom just before serving.

Serves 10.

MIDDLE EASTERN SQUASH SOUP

Squash in this recipe adds flavor and has unmistakable Middle Eastern characteristics.

2 medium onions, diced	1/2 cup Marsala wine
3 garlic cloves, minced	3 cups vegetable stock
1 medium carrot, diced	3 cups squash puree
1 rib celery, diced	1/2 cup cream
1 tsp. whole cumin seed	1/2 tsp. Madras curry powder
1/4 tsp. whole cardamom seed	1/4 tsp. garam masala*
1 tbsp. olive oil	granulated kelp to taste

NOTE: garam masala is Indian equivalent of curry powder. It is a premixed powder consisting of several spicy ingredients. A typical garam masala might include 2 oz. ground coriander seed, 2 oz. ground chile pepper, and pinch of ground black pepper.

Sauté first half-dozen ingredients in olive oil. Then add wine to deglaze. Add stock and squash puree and bring to simmer over medium heat. Then add cream and spices. Simmer for 5 minutes and serve.

Makes 7 1/2 cups.

As a cultivated plant, spinach originated in or near Persia and later reached Spain by way of the Moors around 1100–1200 A.D.

COLD SPINACH SOUP

1 1/2 cups yogurt
1 cup chopped spinach
2 chopped scallions
1/4 cup chopped parsley
3/4 tsp. lemon juice

3/4 tsp. lime juice
1 tsp. tamari
1/2 tsp. kelp
1 mashed garlic clove
dash of paprika for garnish

Put yogurt in blender and then slowly add other ingredients, with blender set on medium speed. Blend until reduced to soupy consistency. Some of spinach will be totally pulverized, while much of it will still be in small bits. The combination of spinach, parsley, and scallions give a real zing to this soup. If it's a bit too zingy for your taste buds, dilute flavor with some more yogurt. Finally, garnish each bowl with a sprinkle of paprika. Other variations are to add 1/2 tsp. of fresh grated ginger root when blending everything up, or replace paprika with a single cross-sectional slice of sweet red pepper instead.

Serves 2.

Watercress soup is one of the most popular folk remedies among Chinese residing in Hong Kong.

WATERCRESS SOUP

1 qt. chicken stock
1 tbsp. honey
1/2 tsp. blackstrap molasses
pinch of kelp

1 bunch watercress
water to cover stems
pinch of cardamom

Heat stock and season with honey, molasses, kelp and cardamom. Before untying bunch of purchased watercress, cut off stems. Wash stems and boil for about 10 minutes. Drain cooking water into stock. (Cooked stems by themselves can be eaten when seasoned with a little tamari soy sauce.)

Wash tops of watercress (flowers) and add to boiling stock just before serving. Boil soup 3 minutes, no longer, as you don't want to lose the emerald green color. Be sure to cook uncovered after you add watercress or it will darken.

Makes 4 cups.

Basic soup stock generally consists of about 50% allium vegetables (onions, leeks, shallots, garlic) and 25% each of celery and carrots, plus herbs, spices and water. Some chefs will add dried or fresh mushrooms or dried beans, but try to avoid vegetables that have a strong dominating flavor, such as broccoli, cauliflower, cabbage and peppers.

HEARTY VEGETARIAN-NUT SOUP STOCK

5 cups unpeeled Bermuda onions, sliced in half-moons

1/4 cup shallots, cut in half

2 cloves garlic

2 large carrots, unpeeled and sliced

4 stalks celery, sliced

1 medium parsnip, sliced

1/2 cup parsnip root, diced

2 medium unpeeled potatoes, sliced

1/4 cup canola oil

1/4 cup sweet rice wine (mirin)

1 gallon water

1/4 cup navy beans, soaked 12 hours, drained

1/4 cup green lentils

1/8 cup chopped walnuts

1/8 cup pistachios

1/8 cup pine nuts

1/8 cup hickory nuts

1 1/2 cups tomatoes, diced

2 tbsp. tamari

6 parsley sprigs

2 bay leaves

1/4 tsp. dried thyme

1/4 tsp. dried rosemary

2 cloves (spice)

8 whole peppercorns

Preheat oven to 450°F. Place onions, shallots, garlic, carrots, celery, parsnips, and potatoes on a large, flat baking sheet and brush with oil. Leave them uncovered while roasting in oven for approximately 1 hr. and 10 minutes or until nicely brown; be sure to turn them every so often with metal spatula.

On separate oiled baking sheet, spread out the different nuts. Put them on lower rack inside oven, but roast for only half the allotted time. Be sure and use only *raw* nuts for this, not any that have been previously roasted and salted in oil. Remove nuts and set aside until vegetables are finished.

Place roasted vegetables and nuts in stock pot with sweet rice wine and 1 cup water. Cook over medium heat until some liquid evaporates. Then add remaining ingredients. Cook uncovered for 1 1/2 hrs. and strain.

Serves 4.

Some years ago, while lecturing among some Amish folks in the rural area just outside Smicksburg, Pennsylvania, I was treated to a very special meal in the home of Amos Yoder and family.

Instead of eating in a fancy, four-star Manhattan restaurant, I ate in a humble abode with simple but genuinely friendly folks, who often used the Bible and prayers as their guides for daily living.

The kudzu plant has a woody stem, broad leaves, and a root 6 to 9 feet in length. It has been gathered since ancient times in both China and Japan from November until April.

CREAM OF BLACK WALNUT SOUP

2 cups black walnuts, chopped
3 tbsp. chopped celery
1 tbsp. chopped chives
5 cups chicken stock
2 tbsp. cream sherry

2 tsp. butter
1 cup heavy cream
pinch salt to taste
grated nutmeg for topping

Combine walnuts, celery and chives with some chicken stock in saucepan. Bring to rolling boil, then move pan to medium heat for 20 minutes. Then stir in sherry, butter, cream and salt with wire whisk. Reheat soup before serving it in individual soup bowls. Ladle some chopped black walnut meats into each bowl and top off with sprinkle of nutmeg.
      Serves 8.

JEWEL SOUP WITH KUDZU

1 1/2 cups dashi*
1 tsp. natural soy sauce
1/2 tsp. granulated kelp
1/2 tsp. sake (Japanese rice wine)

1 tsp. kudzu powder, dissolved in 1 1/4 tbsp. water
6 oz. tofu, drained and cut into 1 1/2" cubes
1/2 leek or 2 scallions, cut into thin rounds
4 slivers of lime peel

Bring the dashi just to a boil over moderate heat. Reduce heat to low, add the next four ingredients and cook, stirring constantly, until soup begins to thicken. Add tofu and simmer until center of tofu is well heated. Remove tofu carefully with a slotted spoon and divide among two soup bowls. Garnish with sliced leeks and lime peel, then carefully pour in the simmer broth.
      Serves 2.
      *All foreign ingredients cited here can be obtained from any Oriental food store in larger cities, especially those catering to Japanese clientele.

This "nautical" soup is considered by some to be an aphrodisiac.

This delightful tea-based soup will keep you healthy all year long.

SARGASSO SEA SOUP

1/2 cup fresh or dried Sargassum (use blades of uppermost fronds only)

8 cups chicken broth

1/2 cup dried nori sheets

1/2 cup dried wakame fronds

1/2 cup small dried shrimp

1/2 cup dried sardines

1/2 cup soy sauce

2 tbsp. sesame oil

NOTE: Various species of *Porphyra* may be substituted; these include purple laver from Scotland, nori from Japan, kim from Korea, chi choy from China, and summer seaweed from the Pacific Northwest. You can find most of these seaweeds in specialty food stores catering to Chinese, Japanese, or Korean cultures as well as general Oriental food stores.

If fresh Sargassum is used, first rinse it under cold water to remove all particles of sand. Boil broth and blanch sea vegetables in it to make them pliable. Remove leaflike blades from Sargassum. Chop nori and wakame and add to boiling broth. Add dried shrimp and sardines. Add soy sauce and sesame oil. Boil gently for about 2 hours or until everything is tender.

Serves 8–10.

BREATHE EASIER SOUP

3 cups Gunpowder green tea

1 onion, finely minced (or 1/4 cup onion flakes)

1 carrot, diced (or 1/4 cup dried or frozen diced carrots)

2 tbsp. yerba mate tea leaves

1/2 tsp. coarse kelp

1/2 tsp. basil

1/2 tsp. oregano

1/2 tsp. parsley flakes

Cook all ingredients together on medium heat, until carrots are done. Discard yerba mate leaves and serve hot.

Serves 4.

Legumes promote vigor and vitality. Make this hearty soup and you will soon regain a radiant glow of health.

LEGUME TEA SOUP

1 cup red peas, dried broad beans, or adkuki beans

1 cup goat's milk

1 cup English Breakfast or Keemun Congou or Lapsang Souchong Tea

3 sprigs fresh thyme, or 3 tsp. dried, or some dill

4 whole allspice berries

1 peppercorn

coarsely granulated kelp for flavor

Wash beans or peas and add to pot. Add milk and tea. Cook legumes until they're soft but not mushy. When cooked, add spices and kelp. Simmer until soft, adding more tea if necessary.

Serves 4.

For cooking purposes, the small sugar pumpkins averaging 7 lbs. or so are best.

PUMPKIN TEA SOUP

2 lb. pumpkin, peeled and chopped into 2" chunks

4 cups spicy Formosa black tea

1/2 lb. sweet potato, chopped

1 scallion, crushed (if allergic, then omit*)

1 clove garlic (if allergic, then omit*)

1 sprig fresh thyme or 1 tsp. dried herb

2 tbsp. barley miso or sea salt to taste

* Dill may be substituted for scallion or garlic if there is an allergy.

In medium-sized saucepan, add pumpkin to 2 cups tea. Cook until pumpkin is soft enough to crush or puree. While pumpkin is cooking, in separate saucepan add sweet potato to 2 cups tea and cook until it's soft but not mushy.

Drain tea, puree sweet potato or mash it with fork, and add it to pumpkin with scallion/garlic and thyme or dill and thyme. Add more tea if mixture is too thick. Add sea salt, if not using miso. Cook for 10 minutes. Take out 1/4 cup soup and dissolve miso in it. Return to pot and heat for 3 more minutes (don't boil).

Serves 4.

An aphrodisiac from France. Just add your love!

BOUILLABAISSE (ORIGINATED IN PROVENCE, FRANCE)

Appr. 7 lbs. various fish

1 fresh lobster, crab or scampi

40 mussels

3 medium-large yellow onions, finely diced

2 fresh fennel flowerheads and leaves, chopped

6 whole tomatoes (fresh or canned)

2-4 crushed garlic cloves

1/2 pint extra virgin olive oil

1/2 pint white wine

4 tbsp. chopped parsley

1 sprig thyme

2 bay leaves

1 large piece dried orange peel

salt and white pepper for taste

saffron

8-16 slices French bread and butter to fry them in

Clean and gut fish. Cut lengthwise and across the crustaceans and crush their claw shells. Remove mussels from their shells. Next, dump the vegetables into the oil in a large stainless-steel pot; cover them with a layer of the firmer fish, pour in wine, and add water enough to cover fish. Then season with salt, pepper and saffron.

Boil with lid on for about 8 minutes, then add less firm fish and boil for another 8 minutes. Strain out fish and crustaceans, laying them on a dish; sprinkle parsley over them and into soup. Meanwhile, the bread slices should have been fried. Pour soup into bowls and put bread slice in each. The rest of the fish can be put on a large platter on the table and some of it cut up and added to the soup by individual diners.

Serves 6.

WEST INDIAN FISH GARLIC SOUP

2 lbs. assorted fresh fish	1/4 tsp. powdered turmeric
1/2 gal. water	2 cloves garlic, finely minced
1 cup white wine	1 tsp. liquid kyolic garlic
1 bay leaf	1 tsp. coarse granulated kelp
1 large onion, peeled and sliced	pinch of cayenne pepper
1/2 cup sliced celery	pinch of powdered thyme
1/2 cup chopped raw carrots	pinch of rosemary
2 large raw potatoes, peeled and chopped	

Clean and cut up fish—rock cod, bass, or whatever is available. Put fish, head and tail in large pot and cover with water. Bring to rolling boil, then add white wine and bay leaf. Simmer until fish falls apart, about 1 1/2 hours. Discard bones, fins, head, and so on.

Sauté celery and onions in butter until golden brown. Pour sauteed vegetables into stock, rinsing pan with some of stock, and add it back into pot for extra flavor and color. Next add carrots, potatoes, seasonings, and liquid kyolic garlic as well as minced raw garlic. Simmer for another hour or until vegetables are mushy.

Remove soup from stove and force everything through a food mill or a large-hole food colander, or blend the entire soup with the vegetables and the fish in a blender, adding a little at a time. Return to pot and bring to another boil. Correct seasonings if necessary. The soup should have the consistency of cream soup, but without benefit of milk, cream, flour, or grease.

Serves 4 to 5.

I love the rich interplay of aromas and spices in this soup.

HOT AND SOUR SHRIMP SOUP

5 cups chicken stock

4 scallions, white and green parts, chopped

2 tbsp. chopped fresh cilantro

1 small fresh hot green chili, seeded and chopped

3 lemongrass stalks, cut into 1-inch pieces

pinch of salt

1-inch piece lime peel

2 tbsp. lime juice

1 lb. shrimp

In saucepan, combine all ingredients except shrimp. Bring to simmer, cover, and cook over low heat for 25 minutes to nicely blend flavors. Strain and discard solids. Return liquid to saucepan, add shrimp, and cook until shrimp are just heated through, no more than 1 1/2 minutes.

Serves 4.

If you begin with fresh ingredients, this soup may be made in advance and refrigerated for up to 2 days.

BLUEBERRY SOUP

2 cups plain yogurt

2 cups orange juice

1 tbsp. honey

1/2 tsp. cinnamon

1 cup frozen unsweetened blueberries, thawed

Garnish: fresh mint sprigs, optional

In a food processor fitted with steel blade, blend together yogurt, orange juice, honey and cinnamon. Fold in blueberries. Serve chilled in cold bowls. Garnish with fresh mint sprigs.

Serves 4.

VARIATION: Omit blueberries, add 1 ripe banana, and puree with other ingredients.

FRESH BLUEBERRY SOUP WITH BLUEBERRY CORN MUFFINS

A delightful—and different—berry recipe

for soup:

2 cups fresh blueberries

1 1/2 cups water

1/2 cup sugar

1/2 tbsp. finely grated orange peel

1/4 cup orange juice

2 cups buttermilk

1 cup sour cream

lemon juice to taste

pinch of nutmeg

Heat berries, water, sugar, orange peel, and juice; bring to boil. Simmer for 15-20 minutes; let cool. Process until pureed in a food blender. Whip in buttermilk and sour cream. Taste for salt and add lemon juice if needed. Chill for two hours. Serve garnished with nutmeg and fresh blueberries.

for muffins:

1 1/3 cups all purpose white flour

2/3 cups yellow cornmeal

1 tbsp. baking powder

1 tsp. ground cinnamon

1/4 tsp. salt

1 cup blueberries

1 egg

2/3 cup skim milk

1/2 cup honey

3 tbsp. extra light virgin olive oil

Preheat oven to 400°F. Lightly brush muffin tin with canola or sunflower oil. In a large bowl, whisk together by hand the flour, cornmeal, baking powder, cinnamon and salt. Add blueberries and toss to coat with flour mixture. In smaller bowl, lightly beat egg. Add milk, honey and oil, whisking until well combined. Add liquid mixture to dry ingredients and stir just until combined. Don't overmix. Divide batter equally among 12 muffin cups, filling each about 2/3 full. Bake for 22 minutes, until well-risen and golden. Turn out onto rack to cool.

Makes a dozen muffins, which is more than enough to go with the fresh blueberry soup.

SALADS

A zesty salad that my family loves.

AVOCADO AND GRAPEFRUIT SALAD WITH POMEGRANATE SEEDS

2 cups loosely packed torn romaine lettuce

2 cups loosely packed torn chicory

2 cups grapefruit sections (about 2 large grapefruit)

1/2 small red onion, sliced and separated into rings

1 medium avocado, peeled and sliced

1 cup pomegranate seeds

2 tbsp. honey

2 tbsp. fresh lime juice

Place 1/2 cup romaine and 1/2 cup chicory on each of 4 salad plates. Divide grapefruit, onion and avocado evenly among plates; top with pomegranate seeds. Combine honey and lime juice, stirring with wire whisk. Drizzle 1 tbsp. of dressing over each salad.

Serves 4.

An attractive salad, unusual, and easy to fix

AVOCADO, CARAMBOLA, AND WILTED SPINACH SALAD

1 tbsp. peanut or corn oil

1 tsp. ground cumin

2 tbsp. chopped red onion

1/3 cup Japanese rice wine vinegar

1 1/2 tbsp. brown sugar

1 tsp. soy sauce

1/4 tsp. red pepper flakes

1 lb. fresh spinach, stemmed, washed, and dried

2 carambolas, thinly sliced

1 avocado, peeled and sliced

In small, heavy skillet heat oil over medium heat, stir in cumin and cook for 30 seconds. Add onions and cook, stirring, until soft, about 2 minutes. Add vinegar, brown sugar, soy sauce, and red pepper flakes, stirring to mix well.

In large bowl toss spinach with 3 tbsp. of warm dressing. Divide salad among 4 plates, arrange carambola and avocado slices over top and drizzle with remaining dressing.

Serves 4.

BEAN SPROUTS SALAD WITH SOY SAUCE DRESSING

for salad:

1 1/2 cups bean sprouts

1 cup carrots

3 green bell peppers

for soy sauce dressing:

1 tbsp. vegetable oil

1 tbsp. sesame oil

3 tbsp. soy sauce

2 tbsp. diluted apple cider vinegar

Mix ingredients for dressing first. Then wash bean sprouts under running water and drain in colander. Cut carrots into 1" long thin strips. Quarter green peppers lengthwise and remove their seeds and ribs. Next, slice each quarter crosswise into long fine strips. Bring to boil 3 1/2 cups water containing 1/4 tsp. salt. Put in carrots and cook 1 minute, then add bean sprouts and green bell peppers. When water simmers again, turn off heat. Drain off water through colander and quickly cool by fanning. Squeeze slightly to remove excess water. Combine all ingredients and mix with dressing just before serving. Arrange in mounds in small salad bowls.

Serves 3.

I'm indebted to Dr. James Duke of Beltsville, MD for letting me feature here a slightly revised version of his Quack Salad.

"QUACK" SALAD

1 cup washed, unpeeled, raw, grated red beets
handful of chopped walnuts (unpackaged, unsalted)
3/4 cup coarsely diced celery
1/2 cup washed, snipped endive
1 medium to large cucumber, washed, unpeeled and sliced
1/4 tsp. cumin

1 tbsp. flaxseed
1 peeled, chopped garlic clove
pinch of powdered cayenne pepper
1/2 peeled, chopped white onion
handful of shelled, chopped peanuts (not canned, salted or fried)
1/2 tsp. sage
2 medium-sized, washed, quartered ripe tomatoes

Lightly toss everything together in large wooden salad bowl until thoroughly mixed. To make dressing, add 1/4 tsp. kelp and 1 finely minced garlic clove to 2 1/2 cups lemon juice. Mix well and pour over salad.
    Serves 2.

I love to prepare this salad in the warmer months of the year.

CABBAGE SLAW WITH BUTTERMILK DRESSING

4 cups thinly sliced red cabbage
4 cups thinly sliced bok choy (Chinese) cabbage
1 cup thinly sliced fresh brussels sprouts
1/4 cup chopped red onion
1/4 cup chopped fresh parsley
1 tsp. sugar
1 tsp. celery seeds

1/2 tsp. salt
1/4 tsp. pepper
1/3 cup low-fat sour cream
1/3 cup nonfat buttermilk
1 tbsp. tarragon white wine vinegar
1 tsp. Worcestershire sauce

Combine first five ingredients in large bowl; toss well, and set aside. Combine remaining ingredients, and stir well. Pour over cabbage mixture; toss gently. Cover and chill 1 hour.
    Serves 8.

Broccoli is a vegetable that is becoming more and more popular every year. It has very high nutritional value.

Broccoli is probably the forerunner of cauliflower and was developed to its high degree of perfection by Danish gardeners. Eat it often!

BROCCOLI SALAD

broccoli flowerets
2 tsp. tarragon vinegar
sea salt and kelp to taste

smidgen of brown sugar
4 tsp. olive oil
1 tsp. tomato puree

Soak broccoli in cold water for 30 minutes. Them break broccoli into flowerets. Tie them loosely in piece of muslin and cook in boiling water for 10 minutes. Drain and chill. Make a dressing of tarragon vinegar, salt, kelp, sugar, and olive oil. Mix well and add tomato puree. Put flowerets in salad bowl and toss gently. If enough broccoli is used, this should serve 4.

SPICY BROCCOLI SALAD

1 1/2 lb. broccoli
3 tbsp. chopped red bell pepper
3 tbsp. chopped red onion
3 tbsp. rice wine vinegar

1 tbsp. sesame oil
2 tsp. light brown sugar
1 tsp. red pepper flakes
granulated kelp to taste

Cut off broccoli florets. Trim and peel stems; cut into 1/2" thick slices. Place broccoli florets and stems in steamer basket over boiling water; cover and steam for 2-3 minutes, or until cooked but still crisp. Refresh under cold water. Drain well. In serving bowl, stir together red peppers, onions, vinegar, oil, brown sugar and red pepper flakes. Just before serving, add broccoli and toss to combine. Season with kelp.

Serves 4.

This quick and easy salad serves as an energy stimulant.

PROTECTIVE CARROT-CABBAGE SALAD

2 1/4 cups finely shredded carrots

2 1/2 cups finely shredded or chopped cabbage

1/3 cup finely chopped green bell pepper

2 tbsp. raisins

3 tbsp. canned pineapple chunks

1 tbsp. pineapple juice from can

1 cup plain yogurt

chopped dates

Mix carrots, cabbage and bell pepper together in large mixing bowl. Add raisins, pineapple chunks, juice and dates. Stir everything together again, mixing well. Finally, turn in yogurt with wooden spoon and mix thoroughly until a smooth, somewhat tight consistency to salad is formed. Serve on romaine lettuce leaves. Or, refrigerate and eat some every day to protect yourself against harmful chemicals in our environment, food, and water supplies.

Serves 6.

Two pieces of lightly buttered pumpernickel toast make a great accompaniment to this salad and warm chicory coffee.

WILTED CHICORY GREENS SALAD

1 medium-sized onion, sliced and separated into rings

1 cup sliced, fresh mushrooms

1 minced clove garlic

2 tsp. butter

1/2 tsp. dried, crushed basil

1/2 cup loosely packed raisins

2 cups endive *

2 cups escarole *

(* snip into pieces with kitchen shears or scissors)

In large saucepan cook onions, mushrooms, and garlic in butter on low heat until tender, but don't brown. Stir in dried basil and a dash of kelp if you like. Then add both kinds of chicory greens and 2 tbsp. of apple cider vinegar. Cook and toss mixture occasionally for 2 1/2 minutes or until greens begin to turn limp or wilty-looking. Just before removing from pan, add raisins and give everything a final stir. Transfer right away to serving dish. Should be eaten relatively soon while still warm.

Serves 4.

Cucumbers have always been credited with being cool and refreshing, not surprising since they are 96% water. Once seen as only a salad ingredient, the cucumber can now also be served as a vegetable in its own right. Delicious salads of cucumber, yogurt and garlic, such as cacik from Turkey and raita from India, are borrowed from Oriental cooking.

A sensational summer treat. I love to serve it for lunch.

THAI CUCUMBER SALAD

1/3 cup minced shallot

1/3 cup sliced green onions

4 medium cucumbers (about 2 1/2 lb.), peeled, halved lengthwise, seeded and thinly sliced

2-4 small red hot chilies, halved lengthwise, seeded and thinly sliced (1-2 tbsp.)

1/2 cup rice vinegar

2 tbsp. brown sugar

1/2 tsp. salt

1/4 cup chopped fresh cilantro

Combine first four ingredients in large bowl. Next combine vinegar, sugar, and salt, and stir well. Add to cucumber mixture, tossing to coat it thoroughly. Stir in cilantro.
Serves 10.

DANDELION, PURSLANE AND CRABMEAT SALAD

3 eggs

2 cups purslane (about 3 oz.), washed, thoroughly dried with paper towel or in vegetable spinner, and chopped medium

1 cup dandelion (about 1 1/2 oz.), washed, thoroughly dried with paper towel or in vegetable spinner, and chopped medium fine

1 tomato cut into 8 wedges

3 oz. cooked king crab meat, broken into bits with all cartilage removed

3 tbsp. mayonnaise

3 tbsp. red wine vinegar

1 tbsp. olive oil

3 tbsp. medium picante sauce

Hard boil eggs, peel and slice them. Combine purslane and dandelion. Place them in center of large plate. Surround with tomato and sliced eggs. Sprinkle crab meat on top. In small bowl thoroughly mix mayonnaise, vinegar, oil, and picante sauce. Pour over greens and crab, and serve.
Serves 4.

Purslane has long been used as a foodstuff in the Middle East. It is incredibly rich in Vitamin C.

GREEK SALAD WITH PURSLANE AND SPAGHETTI

6 oz. spaghetti (a bunch about 2" in diameter)

2 cups purslane flowers, leaves and stems, washed, thoroughly dried with heavy paper towel, and chopped medium fine

1 medium clove garlic, finely chopped

1 cup feta cheese in 1/2" cubes

12 Greek olives, pitted and sliced

4 tbsp. extra virgin olive oil

3 tbsp. lime juice

1/2 tsp. basil

1/2 tsp. oregano

1/2 tsp. salt

granulated kelp

Cook spaghetti, rinse under cold water, then drain and cool. In large bowl combine spaghetti, purslane, garlic, feta cheese, and Greek olives. In smaller bowl combine olive oil, lime juice, basil, oregano, salt, and kelp. Pour over spaghetti and purslane. Mix.

Serves 4.

DILLED GREEN BEAN SALAD WITH CREAMY CUCUMBER SAUCE (ADAPTED FROM COUNTRY JOURNAL, APRIL 1987)

This salad is truly refreshing on a hot day.

for salad:

1 1/2 lbs. green beans

1/2 cup olive oil

1/4 cup tarragon vinegar

1 tbsp. chopped fresh parsley

1 tbsp. fresh chives

1 tsbp. dill weed

kelp to taste

small bunch of watercress

for sauce:

1/2 cup nonfat yogurt

2 tbsp. nonfat dry milk

1 cucumber, peeled, finely chopped

1 clove garlic, minced

1/2 tsp. lemon peel, grated

1 tsp. dried dillweed (or 1 tbsp. fresh dill chopped)

1/2 tsp. salt

Wash and trim green beans. Boil until tender. Rinse under cold water. Drain well, patting dry with paper towel. Whisk together oil, tarragon vinegar, and herbs.

Season to taste with kelp. Pour over beans and stir well. Correct seasonings, if necessary. Chill. Before serving, break watercress into small pieces and toss with green beans. Arrange on platter.

To prepare sauce, whisk together yogurt and dry milk until well blended. Stir in cucumber, garlic, lemon peel, dill and salt. Pour over salad

Serves 6.

Try this tasty salad when you want to eat "light."

"CRISPY-HEAD" LETTUCE WITH VELVET DRESSING

1 wedge of iceberg lettuce (thoroughly rinsed)

1/2 cup sour cream

1/2 cup low-fat or no-fat mayonnaise

2 green onions, minced

2 1/4 tbsp. lime juice

1/8 tsp. grated lime peel

1/2 cup blue cheese, crumbled

pinch of granulated kelp (seaweed from any health food store)

Plunge a cored head of iceberg into a large bowl of cold water. Drain, wrap in towel, and stick in refrigerator overnight.

Next day combine sour cream, mayonnaise, green onions, lime juice, and grated lime peel, and mix everything thoroughly. Stir in cheese; then chill about 5 hours.

To serve, cut lettuce into 2 or 4 large wedges, spoon on this velvety cream dressing, and lightly season with kelp.

Serves 2–4.

The Japanese have over 100 different ways to cook with daikon radish. Raw, it can be grated and eaten with fish or meat. It's used to make flowers for garnish, and is that stringy white stuff that's put with sashimi (raw fish) in Japanese restaurants. Or it can be shredded and dressed with a sweet vinaigrette for a salad.

LATIN LOVER SALAD

1 head romaine lettuce, torn into bite-sized chunks

1 bunch of fresh chopped coriander

1 bunch of thinly-sliced radishes and their leaves

1 chopped green bell pepper (including its seeds)

2 peeled, pitted, and sliced avocados

2 sliced, ripe tomatoes

1/2 lb. shelled, de-veined and boiled shrimp

1/3 cup olive oil

2 de-seeded limes, cut in half

kelp to taste

Arrange vegetables and shrimp in large bowl, and drizzle with olive oil. Squeeze on lime juice and add kelp. Toss lightly. Serves 4–6.

NOTE: Recipe adapted from *Vegetables* by four San Francisco Bay Area writers and courtesy of publisher, Chronicle Books.

RADISH-CABBAGE SLAW WITH SESAME-YOGURT DRESSING

This delightful recipe has all the freshness of a summer garden. I highly recommend it.

2 cups shredded cabbage (preferably mixture of red and green cabbage)	3/4 cup plain yogurt
	2 tsp. chopped fresh dill (or 1 tsp. dried dill)
1 cup grated carrot	1 tsp. sesame seed oil
1 cup grated daikon radish	1/4 cup toasted sesame seeds
2/3 cup grated red radish	1 1/2 tbsp. tamari

In large bowl combine cabbage, carrot, and both kinds of radish. Stir in yogurt, dill, sesame oil, sesame seeds and tamari. Taste and add more tamari if desired.

NOTE: Recipe adapted from *Vegetables* by four San Francisco Bay Area writers and courtesy of publisher, Chronicle Books.

ONCE-A-YEAR SALAD

Another "power eating" recipe that follows the old medical adage, "Food is your best medicine."

4 large vine-ripened tomatoes, blanched in hot water, peeled	1/2 pint virgin olive oil
	1/2 pint red wine vinegar
1 large or 2 small vidalia (sweet) onions	1 tsp. fresh chopped basil
2 cloves garlic	coarsely granulated kelp, to taste

Slice tomatoes thickly and layer with thinly sliced onions. Combine olive oil, vinegar, crushed garlic, chopped basil, and kelp together. Mix well and pour over salad. Marinate in refrigerator for 4 hours. If desired, add quartered radishes, green bell pepper rings (and the chopped inner seed core of the pepper), and finely snipped fresh watercress.

Serves 4.

Watercress is a perennial plant which thrives in clear, cold water and is found in ditches and streams everywhere while the pomegranate grows wild as a shrub in its native southern Asia and in hot areas of the world.

WATERCRESS SALAD WITH TANGELOS AND POMEGRANATE SEEDS

5 tangelos	2 tbsp. red wine vinegar
2 tbsp. minced fresh basil	1 tbsp. walnut or sesame oil
1/4 tsp. pepper	8 cups loosely packed trimmed watercress
1/8 tsp. salt	1 cup pomegranate seeds

Grate 2 tbsp. rind from tangelos. Squeeze 1 tangelo to extract 3 tbsp. juice; discard tangelo. Then combine tangelo rind, tangelo juice, basil, and the next 4 ingredients in large bowl. Cover and let stand 2 hours. Peel and section remaining 4 tangelos; set aside. Stir tangelo juice mixture; add watercress and toss gently. Place 1 cup watercress mixture on each of 8 salad plates; arrange tangelo sections and pomegranate seeds on top of watercress mixture. Serve immediately.
   Serves 8.

This is a salad that can't be beat on a hot summer day!

GUAVA FRUIT SALAD

3 cups shredded cabbage	1/2 cup sliced celery
1 peeled and sectioned orange	1 (8 oz.) carton orange yogurt
1 cup halved seedless red grapes	1 small guava, chopped and with seeds removed

In large salad bowl combine cabbage, orange sections, grapes, and celery. For dressing stir together yogurt and guava. Spread dressing over cabbage mixture. Cover and chill. Just before serving, toss salad gently. Serve on cabbage-lined plates, if desired.
   Serves 10.

The common nasturtium is cultivated in the U.S., along with several other species, as ornamentals for their yellow or red flowers. Some nasturtium plants are occasionally used for food.

NASTURTIUM RICE SALAD

1 clove garlic, crushed

3 tbsp. olive oil

3 tbsp. nasturtium vinegar

3 tbsp. apple juice

1 cup cooked brown rice, cold

1 medium onion, chopped

1 medium green pepper, seeded and sliced

4 slices fresh pineapple, cut into chunks

3 tbsp. cooked sweet corn

1/2 cucumber, diced

nasturtiums to garnish

In small bowl, whisk garlic oil, nasturtium vinegar, and juice together until smooth. In large mixing bowl, toss rice and onion with this dressing. Then stir in pepper, pineapple, corn, and cucumbers. Arrange on glass serving dish with flowers.

Serves 5–6.

To make nasturtium vinegar, cut into small pieces enough nasturtium leaves and flowers to make 1/2 cup. Put this amount into an empty quart glass jar and pour over it 2 1/2 cups apple cider vinegar. Screw on lid and store in cool, dry place for 5 days, shaking contents vigorously several times each day. Strain and store liquid in another bottle for use later on.

Tropical fruits can enliven some otherwise dull dishes; in addition, they enhance digestion.

Cranberries are among my favorite foods; I used this particular recipe years ago when I worked in the food-service business as a chef at a country club restaurant in Utah.

PINEAPPLE-ALMOND TURKEY SALAD

1 pineapple
2 cups cooked, diced turkey (or chicken)
1/2 cup Italian dressing
1 tbsp. soy sauce
1/2 cup toasted, slivered almonds
1 chopped green onion (including stem)
2 thinly sliced celery ribs
1/2 cup seedless grapes

Cut pineapple into halves or quarters, lengthwise. Remove fruit, leaving a half-inch of shell. Drain shells on paper towels. Cut fruit into small chunks. Set aside 1 cupful for salad. Refrigerate remaining fruit to use in another recipe. Combine turkey, dressing, soy sauce, almonds, onion, celery, the reserved pineapple, and grapes. Toss gently to combine, making sure all ingredients are coated with dressing. Divide equally among pineapple shells. Chill for 1 hour.
    Serves 4.

CRANBERRY SALAD

1 envelope Knox unflavored gelatin (stay away from prepared mixes)
1 tsp. lime juice
1 tsp. lemon juice
1 tsp. lime rinds
1 tsp. lemon rinds
1/4 cup cold tonic or spring water
1 (1 lb.) can jellied cranberry sauce
1 medium-sized apple

Soften gelatin in cold water for a couple of minutes and dissolve over hot water. Next mash canned jellied cranberry sauce with a fork and add dissolved gelatin. Refrigerate for awhile. Coarsely grind lime and lemon rinds and entire apple in grinder or Vita-Mix. Just as gelatin mixture begins to gel, stir in citrus and apple. Turn into salad molds and chill until firm.
    Serves 4.

DR. JENSEN'S GREEN DELIGHT SALAD

1 tbsp. unflavored gelatin	1 sprig mint
1 tbsp. cold water	1 leaf lettuce
1/2 cup alfalfa sprouts	some salad dressing (fat-free)
1 cup unsweetened pineapple juice	olives

Soften gelatin in water and then melt mixture over boiling water. Blend in sprouts, pineapple juice, and mint. Then pour gelatin mixture into pineapple juice mixture, and combine them thoroughly. Pour into a wet mold and chill until set. Turn out on bed of leaf lettuce and garnish with some salad dressing (fat-free) and olives.

Serves 2–3.

ROYAL KIWI MOLD

2 cups natural grape juice	1/4 tsp. sea salt
2 tbsp. agar-agar flakes	2 tbsp. kudzu, diluted in 1 cup cold water
1-2 tbsp. pure maple syrup, to taste	2 kiwifruit, peeled and sliced

In large saucepan combine grape juice, 1 cup water, and the agar-agar. Bring to boil, then reduce heat to low and simmer for 5 minutes. Add pure maple syrup and sea salt and bring to boil again, then reduce heat to low and simmer for 10 minutes. Whisk in diluted kudzu and cook over low heat until mixture begins to thicken, about 5 minutes. Pour into glass bowl and arrange kiwi slices around edge and in center of gelatin. Let cool to room temperature, and refrigerate until firm, at least 1 1/2 hours.

Serves 6.

This is the personal health-giving recipe of Dr. Bernard Jensen, a regular participant for many years in several National Health Federation conventions, where he was a popular speaker. I had the pleasure of introducing him to audiences on a few occasions.

Once called Chinese gooseberry, this fruit was brought to New Zealand's North Island where it was widely cultivated and improved upon. American GIs stationed in New Zealand developed a strong tast for kiwifruit and the rest is history.

If you need or want more fish oils in your diet, try this health-gaining salad.

A Mexican plant, the jicama, is usually pickled. The seed pods are rubbed to remove their irritating hairs and then cooked and eaten like snapbeans.

COLD FISH SALAD

4 peeled tomatoes, sliced	1 small can salmon meat
4 boiled potatoes, sliced	1/4 pint apple cider vinegar
2 oz. celery cut julienne (french-fry) style	4 romaine lettuce leaves
1 oz. blanched (in hot water) onion rings	1 hard boiled egg

Mix tomatoes, potatoes, celery, onion rings, and salmon. Blend all of the above with apple cider vinegar marinade. Dress on bed of romaine lettuce. Sprinkle with chopped or julienne of egg.
    Serves 3.

GARDEN-FRESH TUNA SALAD

1 can (6 1/2 oz.) water-packed, low-sodium tuna, drained and broken into chunks	3/4 cup jicama, peeled, julienne-sliced
1/4 cup + 2 tbsp. fat-free bottled Italian dressing	1 cup sugar snap peas, strings removed and halved crosswise
2 cups torn lettuce	1 medium tomato, chopped
2 cups washed and torn fresh spinach leaves	1/2 cup julienne-sliced carrot

Place tuna in shallow, non-metal bowl; pour 1/4 cup Italian dressing over. Refrigerate 15 minutes to 2 hours before assembling salad. To make salad, in large bowl toss together lettuce, spinach, undrained tuna, jicama, sugar snap peas, tomato, and carrot with remaining 2 tbsp. dressing. Serve with corn tortilla chips.
    Serves 3.

One of my favorite dressings, this vinaigrette is sure to please.

SUBTLE LIME LIQUEUR VINAIGRETTE

1 small crushed garlic clove	*1/2 tsp. paprika*
1/2 tsp. kelp	*1/8 tsp. thyme*
2 1/2 tbsp. lime juice	*1/8 tsp. rosemary*
1/4 cup unsweetened apple juice	*1/2 tsp. pure maple syrup*
3 tbsp. of any fruit-flavored liqueur	*2/3 cup pure virgin olive oil*

Mash garlic and kelp to a paste in small bowl using the back of heavy spoon. Add lime juice, liqueur, paprika, thyme, rosemary, and maple syrup, and blend thoroughly. Then gradually whisk in olive oil and apple juice with wire whip until mixture is smooth and thick. Should make enough dressing for 4 whole-meal salads.

Two salad dressings that use grapeseed oil as a healthy alternative for other oils.

MAYONNAISE SUBSTITUTE FOR SALAD GREENS

2 tsp. chopped garlic

1 egg yolk

1 tsp. boiling water

granulated kelp to taste

1 cup grapeseed oil

1 tsp. lemon juice

Add yolk to garlic and beat. Then add water and granulated kelp. Next, add oil and beat. Finally, add lemon juice.

FRESH TARRAGON VINAIGRETTE

1/2 cup fresh tarragon leaves

1/4 cup grapeseed oil

3 tbsp. Dijon mustard

2 tbsp. apple cider vinegar

1/2 tsp. granulated kelp

Whisk together Dijon mustard, vinegar, and kelp. Slowly add grapeseed oil, while whisking, until thick. Add chopped tarragon leaves. Serve over fresh greens.

E N T R E E S

Many people make the mistake of overcooking broccoli, which causes the heads to fall apart and much of its flavor to be lost. It is better to undercook it and serve with a little bit of melted butter and a dash of granulated kelp, a seaweed available from health food stores. Albert Broccoli, who gained fame for fifteen James Bond films produced over the last 25 years, belongs to the famous Italian family which brought the seeds of this now famous vegetable named after them from Italy to America at the turn of the century.

The world's most famous secret agent prefers breakfast to any other meal of the day, according to information scattered throughout all the Ian Fleming and John Gardiner novels. And it seldom varies from the traditional orange juice, strong coffee without sugar, scrambled eggs, toast, and frequently bacon. Occasionally, however, Bond has indulged himself in a little breakfast delight consisting of steamed broccoli and soft-boiled eggs.

AGENT 007'S BROCCOLI HARLEQUIN

1 small head cauliflower
2 small bunches broccoli
4 tbsp. butter
2-3 tbsp. plain yogurt
2 tbsp. grated Parmesan cheese

1/4 tsp. salt*
freshly ground black pepper to taste *
3/4 cup rye or pumpernickel breadcrumbs
*I recommend substituting kelp for salt and pepper.

Break cauliflower into florets and remove most of white stalks. Steam cauliflower 3-4 minutes or until still firm. Steam broccoli for about 6 minutes or until soft enough to puree.

Preheat oven to 350°F. Puree broccoli with butter and yogurt. Lightly grease a 6-cup ovenproof dish with olive oil, mound cauliflower in it and sprinkle with the cheese, salt and pepper (or kelp). Season broccoli puree with salt and pepper (or kelp); then spoon it over cauliflower and sprinkle top with breadcrumbs. Bake for 20 minutes.

Serves 6–8.

A JAMES BOND BREAKFAST

4 stalks broccoli
4 eggs
4-6 tbsp. lime juice

Granulated kelp to taste
Paprika and finely chopped parsley as garnish

Steam stalks of broccoli until tender, and cut into thin strips. Soft-boil eggs for 4 minutes. Lay broccoli strips on plate. Shell eggs and chop them in bowl. Blend in lime juice with kelp to taste. Spread this over broccoli, then garnish with paprika and parsley.

Serves 4.

BRUSSELS SPROUTS AND BROCCOLI FRITTATA

Vegetable cooking spray
1/2 cup chopped onion
1 cup small fresh broccoli florets
1 cup thinly sliced brussels sprouts
1/2 cup diced turkey ham
1 garlic clove, minced

2 eggs
4 egg whites
1/3 cup cooked spaghetti (about 1/2 oz. uncooked)
1/4 cup grated Parmesan cheese, divided
1/4 tsp. crushed red pepper

Coat a large nonstick skillet with cooking spray; place over medium heat until hot. Add onion; saute 3 minutes. Add broccoli, brussels sprouts, ham, and garlic. Sauté 2 more minutes. Remove from heat, and set aside. Then lightly beat eggs and egg whites in a bowl with a whisk; stir in broccoli mixture, pasta, and 2 tbsp. cheese. Recoat skillet with cooking spray; place over medium heat until hot. Pour egg mixture into skillet. Cover, reduce heat to medium-low, and cook 8 minutes or until almost set. Sprinkle with remaining cheese and pepper. Wrap handle of skillet with foil; broil 3 inches from heat 1 minute. Cut into wedges; serve warm.

Serves 4.

Brussels sprouts is one of the older types of vegetable, having been grown in this country for a century and in Europe for probably several centuries.

A refreshing vegetarian stew that will give you lots of energy.

CHICKPEA, MILLET, AND VEGETABLE STEW

for cooking chickpeas:
2 cups dried chickpeas

6 cups water
1/2 tsp. salt (optional)

Wash chickpeas and pick out any stones. Soak for 8 hours in cold water or bring beans and water to boil, cook for 2 minutes, turn off heat, and soak for 2 hours.

After beans swell, add enough water to cover; cook in pressure cooker for 50 minutes, or else simmer on stove for 1 1/2 to 2 hours. Add salt 10 minutes before chickpeas have finished cooking. Pour off excess water before serving. (If desired, reserve water for making soup.)

Serves 4 by itself, or use in following stew recipe.

for cooking millet:
2 cups raw millet grain
3 cups boiling water

3 tsp. butter or sunflower seed oil or olive oil
pinch of salt
pinch of powdered cardamom (optional)

Bring water to boil; then add butter or oil. Next, sprinkle in millet a little at a time. Stir briefly and partially cover. Reduce heat to lowest setting possible. Cook millet for 15-20 minutes *only*. Overcooking tends to make it mushy. Stir with fork halfway through cooking, and again at end. This time the trapped steam should escape; otherwise it will keep cooking millet even after it's removed from direct heat. So fluff it with fork a lot after it's cooked and leave it uncovered. This is the best deterrent to avoid mushiness. Add salt and cardamom *after* it's cooked.

for chickpea-vegetable stew:

2 cups cooked chickpea	3 tbsp. fresh lemon juice
4 cups cooked millet	1 lb. bunch fresh broccoli, chopped
2 tbsp. olive oil	1/2 cup (packed) currants
2 tbsp. butter	kelp to taste
1 cup chopped white onion	cayenne pepper to taste
1 tsp. salt	1/8 tsp. mild paprika
1 lb. fresh mushrooms, chopped	1 1/2 cups coarsely chopped toasted cashews

Cook onion in combined olive oil and butter, with salt, in large, heavy skillet. Keep heat medium-low, and cook for 5 minutes or until onion begins to get tender. Add mushrooms, lemon juice, and broccoli. Cover, and cook over medium-low heat until broccoli is bright green and barely tender (8-10 minutes). Add cooked drained chickpeas and all remaining ingredients, and simmer, covered, for another 6 minutes. Serve over millet. Arrange stew in center of platter, with millet around its edges.

Serves 4.

The use of cardamom can reduce intolerances to wheat and milk. Use this powdered spice in any dish that calls for wheat or milk products.

EGGPLANT BAKE

3 medium eggplants

5 tbsp. olive oil

1 yellow onion, chopped

1 clove garlic, chopped

1 tbsp. butter

1/2 cup seasoned breadcrumbs

2 eggs

1 tsp. ground cardamom

3 drops Tabasco sauce

3/4 cup heavy cream

sea salt to taste

granulated kelp to taste

1 roasted red pepper, peeled and chopped*

(*roast in oven at 375°F. for about 25 minutes)

Preheat oven to 375°F. Trim and halve eggplants lengthwise. Sprinkle with 4 tbsp. olive oil and bake 30 minutes. Then cool. Cook onion and garlic in remaining oil over medium heat until tender. Scrape flesh out of eggplants and coarsely chop. Transfer to strainer to drain bitter juices. Cut skin into lengths 1" wide.

Butter an 8" springform pan. Line bottom and sides with skin strips, being sure to keep shiny side down. Then sprinkle bread crumbs into pan and shake it well so that entire interior surface is adequately coated.

Beat together eggs, cardamom, Tabasco sauce, and cream. Season to taste with sea salt and granulated kelp. Fold in eggplant, onion, garlic, and red pepper. Pour into prepared pan and then bake for 35 minutes. Remove from oven. Cool for 15 minutes, then unmold onto serving platter. Allow to cool for an hour. Serve with chopped fresh tomatoes mixed with olive oil and granulated kelp.

Serves 4–6.

I often serve this dish when company arrives. It's never failed to win new admirers.

MUSHROOM RAGOUT

7-8 ozs. fresh shiitake mushrooms	1 stalk celery, finely chopped
1/2 cup reduced-sodium chicken stock	2 tbsp. dry red or white wine or dry sherry
1/4 tsp. dried rosemary	granulated kelp (seaweed) to taste
1 thick slice bacon, diced (2 oz.)	1 tbsp. chopped fresh parsley

Separate shiitake stems from caps. Rinse stems and slice very thin. Combine stems in small saucepan with stock and rosemary. Simmer, covered, until tender (about 10 minutes); do not drain. Meanwhile, clean caps with soft brush. Break caps into bite-sized pieces or leave whole, as desired.

Cook bacon in 10" heavy skillet over medium-low heat until barely colored. Drain bacon on paper towels. Pour off fat; return bacon to skillet. Add celery and increase heat to medium, stirring until bacon is cooked and celery is softened, or about 2 minutes. Add sliced shiitake stems, cooking liquid, and caps; toss until barely softened, about 1 minute. Cook over medium-high heat until most of liquid evaporates, about 5 minutes. Pour in wine or sherry, increase heat to high, and toss until liquid has almost evaporated, about 1 minute. Season with kelp and sprinkle with parsley.

Serves 2.

NOTE: This recipe serves as a prototype, to be modified as desired; try substituting mushroom stock for wine, thyme for rosemary, or adding garlic or shallots. Also a dash of liquid Kyolic aged garlic extract gives added zest.

CURRIED PUMPKIN AND TOMATOES

A West African-inspired dish, it can be either a vegetarian main dish or an accompaniment to simple roasted meats.

2 tsp. pure virgin olive oil

1 1/2 lbs. pumpkin or squash, peeled and cut into 1" cubes

1 large onion, thinly sliced

1 tomato, seeded and diced

1/4 cup curry powder, preferably Madras

pinch of granulated kelp for flavor

nonfat plain yogurt as garnish

In large nonstick skillet heat oil over medium-high heat. Add pumpkin or squash and cook, stirring occasionally, for 3 minutes. Add onions and cook, stirring often, for another 4 minutes. Then add tomatoes, curry powder and 2 cups water; bring to boil. Reduce heat and simmer, uncovered, until pumpkin or squash is tender, but not mushy, for about 23 minutes. Season with granulated kelp (seaweed) and serve over rice, garnished with dab of yogurt.

Serves 3–4.

Kudzu is one of the fastest growing vines in creation. Under ideal conditions, it is capable of growing a foot a day and up to 100 feet in a season. Kudzu has beautiful wisteria-like flowers that emit a sweet fragrance.

VEGETABLE STEW WITH KUDZU

2 tbsp. sunflower or olive oil

1 clove garlic, crushed

1 small Bermuda onion, diced

1 lb. zucchini squash, cut into pieces 2 1/2" in length and about 1/4" square *

1 cup distilled water

1 tbsp. natural soy sauce

1/2 tsp. grated ginger root

1 1/2 tbsp. kudzu powder, dissolved in 1/2 cup water

(*Bamboo shoots, daikon (Japanese) radish, turnip, burdock root, and cabbage can be substituted for zucchini in nearly equal amounts. Or several such vegetables can be combined together in reduced amounts.)

Heat skillet and coat it with oil. Add garlic and sauté 45 seconds; add onion next and sauté for 1 1/2 minutes. Add zucchini and sauté for 5 additional minutes, or until almost tender. Stir in remaining ingredients and bring to rolling boil. Simmer for 1 1/2 minutes or until thickened to stew consistency.

Serves 4–6.

Tomatoes definitely help promote the health and well-being of one of the body's most important organs, the liver.

ENCHILADA CASSEROLE WITH TOMATO SAUCE

1 chopped onion

1 minced garlic clove

1 chopped green bell pepper

1/2 cup sliced mushrooms

1 recipe basic tomato sauce (see below)

1 tsp. chili powder

1 1/2 cups cooked pinto beans

1/2 cup yogurt

1 cup cottage cheese

8 corn tortillas

1/2 cup grated mozzarella cheese

Sauté onion, garlic, green pepper, and mushrooms until onions are transparent. Add tomato sauce, chili powder, and beans. Heat through. Stir yogurt and cottage cheese together. In 1 1/2-qt. casserole dish rubbed with liquid lecithin (available from any health food store), put layer of tortillas, layer of sauce, sprinkle of mozzarella cheese and layer of yogurt mixture. Repeat until all ingredients are used, ending with layer of sauce. Top with yogurt mixture.

Bake at 350°F. for 15-20 minutes. Serve hot.

Serves 8.

for tomato sauce:

1 cup diced onion

2 minced garlic cloves

1 diced green bell pepper (including seed center)

1 (28 oz.) can stewed tomatoes with liquid

1/2 tbsp. kelp

1/2 tsp. oregano

1/2 tsp. basil

3 tbsp. tomato paste

1/2 cup mushrooms

In a large skillet, sauté onion, garlic and pepper in small amount of olive oil until tender. Stir in stewed tomatoes and mushrooms. Let simmer 10 minutes. Add tomato paste and stir well until sauce thickens. Add kelp, oregano and basil, adjusting amounts for taste.

Best made just before serving; simple, quick, and more interesting than the kind we ate as kids!

MACARONI AND CHEESE WITH VEGETABLES

8 oz. pasta (preferably bow ties or large ribbed macaroni)

3 tbsp. margarine, divided

1 tbsp. unbleached flour

1/2 cup vegetable stock

3/4 cup milk

1/2 cup grated Cheddar cheese (2 oz.)

1/2 cup grated Parmesan cheese (2 oz.)

1 tbsp. chopped fresh parsley

1 tsp. basil

1/4 tsp. paprika

1/4 tsp. black pepper

2 cups broccoli florets

1 medium-size sweet red pepper, coarsely chopped

1 cup sliced mushrooms (3 oz.)

2 scallions, sliced

Garnish: scallion curls, optional

Bring large pot of water to boil; cook pasta until *al dente.*

While pasta is cooking, in medium-sized saucepan, melt 2 tbsp. of margarine. Remove from heat; add flour and stir until blended in. Whisk in stock and milk, stirring over medium heat until mixture comes to boil and thickens. Reduce heat to LOW. Stir in cheeses and seasonings. Continue stirring until cheese is melted. Remove from heat and set aside.

In large skillet, melt remaining 1 tbsp. margarine. Add remaining ingredients. Cook vegetables, stirring constantly, for about 5 minutes, until crisp-tender; reduce heat to LOW. When noodles are done, drain well. Toss with vegetables; stir in cheese sauce. Garnish with scallion curls.

Serves 6.

As a rule, Italians have considerably fewer heart attacks than Americans, although many of them can be somewhat overweight. If anything, then, pasta can be a true life-saver so far as cholesterol goes, and should be included in our diets more often.

PASTA PRIMAVERA

1 tbsp. olive oil

1 clove minced garlic

1/2 chopped medium onion

2 large chopped tomatoes

1/2 tsp. oregano

1/4 tsp. marjoram

1/2 tsp. kelp

1/2 cup white wine

1 tbsp. olive oil

2-3 cups favorite sliced vegetables (broccoli, carrots, zucchini, summer squash, etc.)

1 lb. hot, cooked pasta of your choice

grated Parmesan cheese, if desired

Heat 1 tbsp. olive oil in sauté pan. Add garlic and onion; cook until translucent. Stir in tomatoes, oregano, marjoram, and pepper; sauté 2 minutes.

Add wine, let simmer while preparing vegetables. In separate pan, heat 1 tbsp. olive oil. Add vegetables and cook until crisp/tender. Add tomato-onion mixture and serve over hot, cooked pasta. Sprinkle with grated Parmesan cheese if desired.

Serves 3–4.

Two vegetables are called artichokes, but have absolutely no relation to each other. The globe artichoke is a green vegetable somewhat like a tiny cabbage while the so-called Jerusalem artichoke isn't really an artichoke and has nothing to to with Jerusalem—it came to the U.S. from South America. The prized part of the artichoke is its tender heart, used here as a pizza topping.

ARTICHOKE AND SUN-DRIED TOMATO PIZZA

1 package dry yeast

1/2 cup warm water (105° to 115°F.)

1 1/2 cups all-purpose flour, divided

1/4 tsp. salt

vegetable cooking spray

3 tbsp. sun-dried tomato tidbits

1/4 tsp. oregano

1/4 tsp. dried basil

1/8 tsp. salt

1/8 tsp. coarsely ground pepper

1 (14 1/2 oz.) can (no-salt-added) stewed tomatoes, undrained and chopped

1 garlic clove, minced

1 1/2 tsp. cornmeal

3/4 cup drained, coarsely chopped canned artichoke hearts

1 cup (4 oz.) shredded Italian provolone cheese

Dissolve yeast in warm water in large bowl and let stand for 5 minutes. Stir in 1 1/4 cups flour and salt to form soft dough. Turn dough out onto lightly floured surface. Knead until smooth and elastic (5 minutes) and add enough remaining flour, 1 tbsp. at a time, to prevent dough from sticking to hands. Place dough in large bowl coated with cooking spray, turning to coat top. Cover and let rise in warm place (85°F.) free from drafts, 1 hour or until doubled in bulk.

Combine tomato tidbits and next 6 ingredients in small saucepan; bring to boil. Reduce heat and simmer, uncovered, 20 minutes, or until reduced to 1 1/3 cups, stirring occasionally. Remove from heat; let cool. Punch dough down, and roll into 12" circle on lightly floured surface. Place dough on 12" pizza pan coated with cooking spray and sprinkled with cornmeal. Crimp edges of dough with fingers to form a rim. Cover; let rise in warm place 30 minutes. Spread tomato mixture evenly over prepared crust, and top with artichoke hearts and cheese. Bake at 500°F. for 12 minutes on bottom rack of oven. Remove pizza to cutting board, and let stand for 5 minutes.

Serves 6, 1 wedge each.

First domesticated in Southeast Asia, the eggplant is technically considered a fruit, not a vegetable.

EGGPLANT PIZZA

1/4 cup olive oil

2/3 cup warm water

2 cups multigrain biscuit mix (from any health food store)

2 tbsp. stoneground cornmeal (from any health food store)

1 cup natural spaghetti sauce

1 tsp. oregano

1 1/2 tsp. dried basil

1 finely minced garlic clove

1/4 cup shredded mozzarella cheese

1/2 cup shredded goat cheese (from local deli)

1/4 cup grated Parmesan cheese

1 cup thinly sliced eggplant

Preheat oven to 500°F. Place oil and water in large mixing bowl and stir in biscuit mix. Scrape dough onto pastry board or other flat surface that has been sprinkled with additional biscuit mix. Knead for about 2 minutes, gradually adding cornmeal until dough is smooth and elastic. If dough seems dry, add a few drops of olive oil.

If using a cookie sheet, rub it with olive oil before rolling out dough into circle or any shape you desire. Prior to adding topping, spread thinly sliced eggplant on another cookie sheet, lightly brush with olive oil, and broil in oven for a couple of minutes. Then remove and place them immediately on top of pizza dough. Next spread on spaghetti sauce and sprinkle with oregano, basil, and garlic.

Distribute cheeses evenly over entire surface. Bake for 10–15 minutes until sides and bottom of crust are golden brown and cheese has pretty well melted.

Preparation time is 20 minutes; baking time is 10–15 minutes.

Serves 3–4.

Better for you by far than those at the local McDonald's, Wendy's or Burger King!

Includes healthy, wholesome, and delightful-to-eat seeds in a refreshingly different vegetarian burger recipe.

SPROUT BURGERS

1 cup barely sprouted wheat sprouts
1 cup adzuki bean sprouts
1/2 cup soybean sprouts
1/2 cup pea or lentil sprouts
1 medium onion

1 egg, well beaten
1/2 cup milk
2 tbsp. wheat germ
granulated kelp to taste

Grind sprouts and onion together. Put them in bowl. Add egg, milk, wheat germ, and granulated kelp. Mix thoroughly, using more milk if necessary. Shape into patties with both hands and put on lightly greased baking sheet. Broil until brown but not dried out. Serve as you would any burger. If you don't have exact kinds of sprouts called for, substitute what you do have in roughly the same quantities.

Serves 2–4.

McSUN BURGERS*

1/2 cup grated raw carrots
1/2 cup finely chopped celery
2 tbsp. chopped onion
1 tbsp. chopped parsley
1 tbsp. chopped green pepper
1 beaten egg

1 tbsp. oil
1/4 cup tomato juice
1 cup ground sunflower seeds
2 tbsp. wheat germ
1/2 tsp. salt
1/4 tsp. basil

Preheat oven to 350°F. Combine ingredients and shape into patties. Arrange in oiled, shallow baking dish. Bake in moderate oven until brown on top; turn patties and bake until brown. Allow about 15 minutes of baking for each side. Serves 4.

*Gratitude to Rodale Press for this recipe from its *Rodale Cookbook* and *Natural Healing Cookbook*.

Try this exotic dish when you want a change of pace.

STUFFED CABBAGE ROLLS

24 small or 12 large cabbage leaves

12 oz. lean mutton or panir (Indian cream cheese)

4 oz. ghee

2 oz. onions, finely chopped

6 cloves garlic, chopped

1 oz. ginger

6 green chilies

2 tsp. sea salt

3/4 tsp. cayenne pepper

1/2 tsp. garam masala

1 tsp. flour

little lime juice

1/4 tsp. white pepper

1/4 tsp. red pepper

8-12 oz. tomato puree

Wash cabbage, carefully separate leaves, and simmer in boiled salted water until they are half-cooked. Remove from water and drain. Mince raw meat or panir (cream cheese). Heat some ghee and fry lightly finely chopped onions, 6 chopped garlic cloves, 1/2 oz. ginger, and 3 chilies. Add minced meat or panir, sea salt, cayenne, and garam masala. Cook until tender. Remove from heat, cool, and divide into 12 equal parts. Remove hard stems from cabbage leaves and spread leaves on table. (If leaves are small, place two of them with their edges overlapping on each other.)

Put one part of minced meat mixture on one edge of each leaf; roll and turn sides gently in. Sprinkle over them a little fresh lime juice, salt, white and red pepper; then roll in dry flour and brown in hot butter or ghee.

Remove from ghee and lightly brown in hot butter or ghee remaining onions, ginger, and green chilies. Add rolls along with 2 tsp. water. Cook covered until tender. When nearly done, add tomato puree and cook uncovered for 10 minutes. Add salt and pepper to taste. Serve hot.

Serves 4 to 6.

RACK OF LAMB DIJON

2 racks of lamb (French trimmed by butcher)

Dijon mustard

10 oz. fresh breadcrumbs

2 oz. melted margarine

1 tsp. dried rosemary

1 tsp. chopped parsley

1 tsp. finely chopped garlic

1/4 tsp. thyme

mint jelly

Use enough Dijon mustard to coat meat side of lamb racks. Mix together margarine, spices, and breadcrumbs. Then pack mixture on top of Dijon-covered lamb and roast in oven at 375°F. for about 25 minutes (or until medium rare). To serve, just slice down between bone to have individual chops.

Serves 4.

PEANUT CHICKEN DIJON

1 medium red or green pepper, cut into strips

5 tsp. peanut oil

1 lb. boneless chicken breasts, cut into thin strips

1/4 cup Dijon mustard

2 tbsp. dry white wine

1/4 tsp. cornstarch

3 tbsp. dry-roasted, unsalted peanuts, chopped

2 cups hot cooked rice

In large skillet over high heat, cook peppers in oil until tender-crisp. Add chicken and sauté just until white. Remove from pan; keep warm.

Blend mustard, wine, and cornstarch; add to skillet. Cook over medium-high heat, stirring constantly until mixture thickens. Return chicken and peppers to pan; cook with sauce 3-4 minutes or until heated through. Stir in peanuts. Serve over rice.

Serves 4.

During the summer of 1980 I was privileged to visit what was then called the People's Republic of China. I was one of several different faculty advisers accompanying about 29 third- and fourth-year med students with the American Medical Students' Association to this part of the world to learn more about traditional Oriental medicine. We were served this dish, and it tasted so good that I asked one of our interpreters to get the recipe for me from the chef.

SICHUAN CHICKEN WITH GINGKO NUTS

12 oz. fresh or canned ginkgo nuts

1 to 2 1/2 lb. chicken

3 green onions

6 slices fresh ginger

2 tbsp. rice wine or dry sherry

pinches of salt and white pepper to taste

Soak fresh ginkgo nuts in boiling water, then drain and scrape off skin. Pick off two ends, push bitter core through with toothpick, then soak again.

Blanch chicken in boiling water, then hold beneath cold running water to rinse. Drain and place breast facing upward in casserole dish. Add remaining ingredients except for gingko nuts. Cover with water, bring to boil, reduce heat and simmer for 15 minutes. Turn chicken over, add nuts and continue to simmer until chicken is completely tender.

Remove chicken and cut in half lengthwise, then cut meat diagonally from center into slices. Arrange in its original shape on serving plate. Lift ginkgo nuts from stock with slotted spoon, arrange around chicken and serve at once.

Serves 4.

SOUTHERN CHICKEN GUMBO

1 (2 1/2 lb.) chicken

3 tbsp. flour

3 tbsp. butter

1 tsp. brown sugar

1/2 chopped, sweet red pepper

4 cups cut okra

1 large can tomatoes or 5-6 ripe, skinned tomatoes

1 can corn, or niblets or kernels cut from 3 ears of fresh corn

2 sprigs chopped parsley

2 snipped basil leaves

Simmer chicken in water to cover for 1 hour. Remove chicken from stock and cool, retaining stock. Skin chicken and pick meat from bones. Cut chicken into bite-sized pieces. Brown flour in butter, add sugar, vegetables, and chicken stock. Simmer until tender and gumbo is thick. Add cooked and cut chicken and serve hot.

Serves 2–3.

A unique recipe of former "P.M.Magazine" chef and famous California restaurateur, LaMont Burns, in his book, Down Home Southern Cooking, *(reprinted here with permission of publisher, Doubleday)*

A delicate entree that's easy to prepare and sure to please.

TAKENOKO GOHAN (BAMBOO RICE)

1/2 lb. bamboo shoots
1/2 lb. boned chicken leg, with skin
3 1/3 cups short-grain rice, washed

for boiling rice:
4 cups chicken stock
1 tsp. granulated kelp
2 tbsp. light soy sauce
2 tbsp. sake
1/2 sheet toasted nori seaweed

Halve canned bamboo shoots lengthwise and wash thoroughly. Cut into half-moon slices. Wash again and drain in colander. Parboil them for 2 minutes, then rinse again in cold water. Drain. Next debone chicken leg, cut meat into 1/2" cubes, parboil for 2 minutes, and wash in cold water to eliminate excess fat. Drain.

Next put washed rice into heavy, tight-lidded pot. Mix liquid for boiling it and pour over rice. Stir in bamboo and chicken. Cover and bring to boil over medium heat, then raise heat to high and cook until most of liquid is absorbed. Reduce heat to very low and cook, covered, until all liquid is absorbed (about 25 minutes). Turn off heat, line underside of pot lid with kitchen towel, cover, and let rest about 15 minutes before serving. To serve, gently fluff rice with wooden spoon and serve in individual bowls. Garnish with crumbled toasted *nori* seaweed available from any Oriental food store.

Serves 4.

CUMIN-FLAVORED GAME HEN

In some ways cumin seeds resemble car-away seeds, but are lighter in color and bristly instead of smooth, and almost straight instead of being curved. Cumin brings out flavor in game fowl like Cornish hens and pheasants.

2 Cornish game hens (about 3 lbs. total)	*2 tbsp. olive oil*
2 tsp. sea salt	*1 tbsp. apple cider vinegar*
1 tsp. brown sugar	*1/2 cup flour*
1/2 tsp. anise seed	*1/4 cup olive oil*
1/4 tsp. ground ginger	*1 1/2 cups hot distilled or spring water*
2 medium bay leaves	*1 tsp. ground cumin*
2 tbsp. soy sauce	*4 cups hot cooked wild rice*

Wash game hens; cut each in half. Place in shallow dish. Combine next 8 ingredients; bring to boil. Pour over hens. Cover dish; refrigerate several hours or overnight. When ready to cook, remove hens from marinade, reserving it. Dredge hen pieces in flour to coat. Heat 1/4 cup oil in large skillet over medium heat. Add hen pieces, skin-sides down. Cook until browned, turning once. Add water to marinade and pour over hens. Cover; simmer over medium-low heat 25 minutes. Last, add cumin 7 minutes before cooking time is up. Serve hot over wild rice.

Serves 4.

A zesty stew I love to serve to guests!

TURKEY-VEGETABLE STEW

1/2 cup all-purpose flour, divided

1 1/2 lb. turkey tenderloin, cut into 1" pieces

vegetable cooking spray

1 tbsp. vegetable oil

1/2 cup chopped onion

2 (13 3/4 oz.) cans no-salt-added chicken broth

2 cups cubed, peeled kohlrabi

1 1/2 cups coarsely chopped cabbage

1 cup sliced carrot

6 small red potatoes, peeled and quartered

1/2 tsp. dried thyme

1/2 tsp. rubbed sage

2 cups small fresh broccoli florets

2 (14 1/2 oz.) cans salt-free or no-salt-added whole tomatoes, drained and coarsely chopped

1/2 cup water

1 tsp. granulated kelp

Place 1/4 cup flour in large zip-top heavy-duty plastic bag. Add turkey; seal bag and shake well to coat. Evenly coat cast-iron Dutch oven with cooking spray; add vegetable oil and place over medium-high heat until hot. Add turkey and onion; cook 6 minutes or until turkey loses its pink color. Add chicken broth; cook, stirring constantly, to scrape browned bits from bottom of pan. Add kohlrabi and next 5 ingredients; bring to rolling boil. Cover, reduce heat, and simmer 20 minutes or until potato is tender. Add broccoli and tomatoes; cook, uncovered, 5 minutes or until broccoli is tender.

Place remaining 1/4 cup flour in bowl. Gradually add 1/2 cup water, stirring with wire whisk until blended, and add to stew. Stir in kelp (seaweed). Cook over medium heat for 5 minutes, or until thickened, stirring frequently.

Serves 4–8.

PARSLEY AND GREEN ONION RICE WITH FISH

3 cups uncooked rice

warm water

kelp

2 bunches chopped green onions

2 bunches chopped parsley

3 lbs. fish fillets

sea salt as needed

pinch of turmeric

2 tbsp. butter

Rinse rice several times until water is clear; soak in warm water with salt added. Bring large pot of water to boil (about 8 cups). Drain water from soaked rice and add rice to boiling water. Boil about 10-15 minutes until rice is not crunchy but still quite firm. Stir occasionally to prevent grains from sticking together.

Drain rice in strainer; add chopped onions and parsley. Pour cold water over rice, parsley, and onions. Cover bottom of pot with butter and some water. Sprinkle rice and these two vegetables into pot, a spoonful at a time, keeping them in center of pot so as not to touch sides. Cover pot lid with paper or dish towel and place lid tightly on pot. Cook approximately 10 minutes over medium heat; then reduce heat to low. Allow rice to steam 30-40 minutes.

Cut fish into serving pieces; sprinkle with sea salt, kelp, and a bit of turmeric. In skillet, brown fish, cooking until done on both sides in butter. Serve with rice.

Serves 4–5.

GROUPER/RED SNAPPER FRANCAISE

2 lb. grouper or snapper fillet (boneless/skinless)   3 eggs, beaten
1 cup all-purpose flour   lemon/lime wedges
1 teaspoon salt   1/2 cup (1stick) margarine
1/2 teaspoon black pepper

Dredge fish fillets in seasoned flour, then in beaten egg. Heat margarine in skillet, making sure it is hot before adding fish. Fry until golden brown on both sides. Serve with lemon or lime wedges. Top with Sauce Provencal.

Serves 2–3.

Chef Paul Buck notes: "This is a nice, light recipe for the 'fried fish lover' as the egg acts as a gossamer skin. The fish does not absorb the grease like normal fried fish. You may top this fish with any of your favorite sauces or use my own Sauce Provencal."

SAUCE PROVENCAL

1 1/2 lbs. vine-ripened tomatoes, blanched, peeled, seeded   1/2 cup dry white wine
1 cup chopped onions or shallots   1 bay leaf
1 clove garlic   1 tbsp. virgin olive oil
1 sprig thyme   salt and pepper to taste

Sauté onions and garlic together until tender, but do not brown. Add diced tomatoes, thyme, bay leaf, and white wine. Simmer until tender (about 30–35 minutes). Add salt and pepper to taste. Top off any cooked fish with this sauce.

This sauce is a summer-time favorite of mine.

BROILED SALMON WITH PASSION FRUIT SAUCE

A zesty, healthy meal that I never tire of serving.

4 passion fruits

1 tsp. cornstarch

1/8 tsp. cayenne pepper

1/4 tsp. salt

1/4 cup fresh orange juice

1/4 cup diced red onion

1 tbsp. light rum

1/2 tsp. sugar

1 1/4 lbs. skinless salmon fillet, cut into 4 equal portions

3 tsp. vegetable oil

2 small pickling cucumbers, skin peeled in alternating strips, sliced

1 bunch watercress, trimmed, washed, dried (about 2 cups)

1 tsp. balsamic vinegar

Cut tops from passion fruits; scrape out all pulp into container of Vita-Mix or similar food processor. Process pulp until liquified, then strain through sieve to remove seeds. If you do this by hand, just work pulp through sieve, pressing hard with back of wooden spoon to separate pulp from seeds. Set juice and seeds aside.

In small bowl, combine cornstarch, 1/8 tsp. cayenne pepper, and 1/4 tsp. salt. Gradually stir in orange juice, onions, rum, and passion fruit juice. Add sugar and additional cayenne pepper to taste. Set salmon fillets in shallow dish and cover with passion fruit mixture. Cover; marinate in refrigerator for 20-30 minutes, spooning liquid over occasionally.

Preheat broiler and broiler pan. Remove salmon from marinade, reserving marinade. Brush salmon and broiler pan with 2 tsp. of oil. Broil salmon until opaque, about 8 minutes.

Meanwhile, combine reserved marinade and 2 tbsp. water in small saucepan; bring to boil over high heat. Boil 1 minute; remove from heat and season to taste with salt and cayenne pepper. If you like, stir a spoonful or two of passion fruit seeds back into sauce for contrast and crunch.

Just before serving, toss cucumbers and watercress in large bowl with balsamic vinegar, the remaining 1 tsp. oil, and salt to taste. Transfer greens to platter, set salmon on top and spoon sauce over salmon.

Serves 4.

SIDE DISHES

Fennel has been used with all kinds of fish dishes since the time of the Norman conquest of England—and it still is today. It goes equally well with pork, veal in soups, vinaigrette sauces, salads—and artichokes.

Spice up your life a little with this very tasty dish.

ARTICHOKES WITH FENNEL

3 large artichokes, trimmed and halved	2 tbsp. olive oil
4 lemons, halved	2 tbsp. nonfat yogurt
2 bulbs fresh fennel, cored and sliced (about 4 cups)	granulated kelp to taste

Squeeze 2 lemons on artichokes and rub them well with lemon halves. In large steamer or pressure cooker, steam artichokes for 1/2 hr. (but only 6 minutes in pressure cooker), or until slightly tender. Steam fennel for 5 minutes. Let cool slightly and use spoon to remove choke from center of artichokes. Squeeze remaining lemons into a blender and combine with half of fennel, oil, yogurt, and granulated kelp until creamy. Chop remaining fennel and mix with fennel sauce. Spoon this mixture into artichoke halves and serve warm or chilled.

Serves 6.

WHOLE BLACK BEANS

8 oz. whole black beans	4 dried red chilies
2 pints water	12 finely cut cloves of garlic
2 1/2 to 3 tsp. sea salt	1/2 oz. clarified butter (ghee)
1 oz. finely cut ginger root	

Remove grit from beans and wash them 3 or 4 times. Boil water and add salt, beans, garlic, ginger, red chilies, and butter. Cover with lid. When it comes to a boil, reduce heat and simmer 3–4 minutes.

Serves 2–4.

BRAISED RED CABBAGE

3/4 lb. red cabbage	2 oz. butter
1/4 pint apple cider vinegar	4 oz. cooking apples
1/2 oz. brown sugar (or 1 tsp. honey)	pinch of kelp (seaweed)

Quarter, trim and shred cabbage. Wash well and drain, retaining some stock; then season with coarse kelp. Place in well-buttered, ovenproof casserole pan. (Do not use aluminum or iron.) Add vinegar and cover with buttered piece of paper and lid. Bake in moderate oven for approximately 1 1/2 hours. Add peeled, cored apples diced into 1/2" pieces. Recover the lid and continue cooking until tender, about 2 hours total. If a little dry, use stock to moisten.
  Serves 3.

Cabbage is believed to have originated in Northern Europe and seems to have spread southward and eastward into the Mediterranean basin.

BAKED CARROTS

8 carrots, washed and cut into strips	2 tbsp. oil
1/2 cup chopped onion	2 tbsp. lemon juice
1/2 cup raisins	1/2 tsp. cinnamon
1 apple, cored and cut into cubes	1/4 tsp. cloves
2 tbsp. honey	1/2 cup Granola

Place all ingredients in shallow casserole, cover tightly and bake at 375°F. for 45 minutes.
  Serves 6.

Carrots around the world grow in all shapes and colors. Westerners mistake the Asian-types, with their bulbous purplish red roots, for beets. Other colors are pale and deep yellow, red, and white.

Quick and easy to make . . . the toasted almonds make it into a real treat.

CREAMED CELERY WITH ALMONDS

8-10 celery branches with leafy tops intact

1 tbsp. diced shallots (an onionlike plant)

3 tbsp. butter

1/4 tsp. sea salt

1 tbsp. whole wheat flour

1/2 cup cream

1/2 cup chicken broth

1 cup toasted almonds

Slice celery on diagonal; melt butter in heavy pan with tight-fitting lid. Add shallots first, then celery. Cover pan; cook until celery is tender, about 8 minutes. You should not have to add liquid. Shake pan every now and then to prevent scorching. When celery is tender, add sea salt and sprinkle in flour. Toss celery with mixing spoon to distribute flour.

Place pan over a double boiler; add cream and chicken broth. Cook until raw flour is gone, and mixture thickens slightly, about 5 minutes. Add 3/4 cup toasted almonds and toss. Place celery mixture in serving dish; top with remaining almonds. Sprinkle paprika over top and serve.

Serves 3–4.

CURRIED CHICKPEAS AND BLACK BEANS

2 tsp. olive oil

1 cup chopped onion

1 tbsp. minced peeled ginger root

2 tsp. curry powder

1 (14.5 oz.) can diced tomatoes, undrained

1/2 tsp. granulated kelp

1 (15 oz.) can black beans, rinsed and drained

1 (15 oz.) can chickpeas (garbanzo beans), rinsed and drained

1/2 cup chopped fresh parsley

1 tbsp. lime juice

Heat olive oil in large nonstick skillet over medium heat. Add onion and ginger root; sauté 3 minutes or until tender. Stir in curry powder; cook an additional minute. Then add tomatoes; cook another minute, or until mixture is slightly thickened, stirring occasionally. Add kelp, black beans, and chickpeas; stir well. Cover, reduce heat, and simmer 5 minutes. Remove from heat; stir in fresh parsley and lime juice. Serve warm.

Serves 4, 1 cup each.

NETTLE GREENS, GEORGIA-STYLE

2 qts. stinging nettles

3/4 cup stock from boiled chicken wings, and chopped, cooked meat from those wings

3 sliced green onions

2 hardboiled eggs

1/4 tsp. lemon juice

Snip greens into bite-sized pieces. Put in pan with other ingredients except eggs. Simmer on low heat for 20 minutes.

Remove and serve, topped with sliced hardboiled eggs. Season to taste with a little kelp, if needed.

Serves 4.

Chickpeas are ideal meat substitutes and are "unexcelled meat stretchers"; also help to maintain energy and strength for those who wish to reduce their intake of red meat.

Euell Gibbons once wrote that "stinging nettle is very efficacious in removing unwanted pounds!" Those obese individuals who've written to me in the past, desperate for advice on how to reduce and whom I've put on a semidiet of stinging nettle have reported up to 32 1/4 pounds lost in just 3 months or less!

Chickweed begins its growth in the fall and thrives through the sleet and snowstorms of winter, even in the far north.

This recipe, both a fatigue fighter and a cleanser, comes from La Rene Gaunt's cookbook Recipes to Lower Your Fat Thermostat *and is reprinted here with the permission of her publisher.*

CHICKWEED AND CHEESE SOUFFLE

2 tbsp. butter
2 tbsp. whole wheat flour
1 cup milk
1/2 cup chickweed, washed and finely chopped (tightly packed)

1/2 cup cheddar cheese, grated
1/2 tsp. salt
1/4 tsp. white pepper
3 egg yolks
5 egg whites

Preheat oven to 350°F. In a 2–3 qt. saucepan, melt butter over low heat, and when foam subsides, add flour. Cook for a minute or two, stirring constantly. Gradually add milk, stirring constantly, and allow just to begin to boil. Remove from heat and add chickweed, cheese, salt, pepper, and egg yolks. Mix thoroughly.

Immediately before baking beat egg whites and then gently fold into chickweed mixture. Pour souffle mixture into a 1-qt. souffle dish or equivalent-size casserole. Bake in middle of oven for 30 minutes or until souffle is risen, browned, and set.

Serves 2–4.

PERFECT PARSNIP PATTIES

6 cooked parsnips
1/4 tsp. powdered cardamom
1/4 tsp. powdered mace

2 tbsp. whole wheat flour
1/2 cup plain yogurt

Wash, peel and quarter parsnips. Remove core and discard. Cook them in boiling water for 15 minutes until tender. Drain and mash. Use cooking water to adjust consistency. Season with spices. Whisk flour into yogurt. Stir into seasoned parsnips. Shape into 8 patties and brown slowly on nonstick griddle or frying pan. Turn just once. They should have a crisp crust. (Liquid lecithin from any local health food store can be used in place of oil for griddle or frying pan.)

Serves 5.

POTATO LATKES

3 tbsp. canola oil

5 Idaho russet potatoes, peeled

3/4 cup finely chopped red onion

1/4 cup all-purpose white flour

1 tsp. salt

1/4 tsp. freshly ground black pepper

1 large egg, lightly beaten

1 large egg white, lightly beaten

Set oven racks at middle and lower positions; preheat oven to 450°F. Prepare 2 baking sheets by brushing each one with 1 tsp. of canola oil. Using a hand grater, grate each potato. Place them in large bowl and add onions, flour, salt and pepper; toss with 2 forks to mix well. Then add egg, egg white, and remaining 1 tsp. oil and toss to mix. Drop rounded tablespoonfuls of potato mixture onto prepared baking sheets and press lightly to form cakes. Bake for 12 minutes, or until they are golden brown at bottom. Then flip latkes over, switch position of each baking sheet in oven, and continue baking for another 6 minutes, or until golden brown. After they're done, transfer to a platter, arranging latkes browned-side-up, and serve. Latkes may be prepared and stored, covered, in refrigerator overnight, if desired. Reheat them at 350°F. for 12 minutes.

Serves approximately 24.

Modern potatoes fall into three general groups: new potatoes, all-purpose potatoes like the pontiac, and the famous Idaho, or russet, which are used here.

Try this health-giving dish whenever you need a pick-me-up.

POTATO, TOMATO, AND ONION CURRY

1 lb. small red potatoes, cut in half

1 lb. tomatoes

2 tsp. coarsely granulated kelp

pinch of cayenne pepper

1/2 tsp. turmeric

1/3 cup ghee (clarified butter)

8 oz. small whole onions

1/2 tsp. garam masala (available from any specialty food store carrying Indian foods)

3 green chilies, sliced into rings

1 tbsp. minced ginger root

1/2 tsp. honey

Heat the ghee. Skin onions and, keeping them whole, cook over low heat until browned, about 20 minutes, stirring occasionally. Then add potatoes, kelp, cayenne pepper, and turmeric. Cover and cook over low heat, stirring occasionally, until potatoes are nearly cooked, about 30 minutes. Add sliced green chilies, ginger, and honey. Cook and stir over medium-high heat until chiles are tender, about 5 minutes. Stir in tomatoes; cook until heated through. Serve sprinkled with garam masala and chopped fresh parsley.

Serves 4.

FRIED POTATO CURRY

1 1/2 lb. potatoes
4 oz. grated onions
10 cloves garlic
1/2 tsp. turmeric powder
1 tsp. white cumin seeds
1 tbsp. coriander seeds
12 peppercorns
1/2 oz. almonds
2 tsp. salt
1/2 pint yogurt
1/2 tsp. garam masala
1 lb. ghee

1/2 oz. fresh ginger root
1 tsp. cayenne pepper
1 tsp. poppy seeds
6 cloves
2 brown cardamoms
1/2 oz. desiccated coconut
5 green cardamoms
pinches of nutmeg and mace to taste
1/4 pint water
1 tsp. chopped fresh coriander leaves or parsley sprigs
2 finely cut green chilies

Select potatoes that are size of walnuts. Peel and prick all over with fork and soak in 1 1/4 pints ice water and 1 tsp. salt for 30 minutes. Dry them with clean cloth. Heat 1 lb. ghee and fry potatoes on medium heat until brown. While potatoes are frying, roast coriander seeds on a hot griddle and sift skins. Likewise roast poppy seeds, coconut, cumin seeds, cloves, peppercorns, brown cardamoms, the mace, and nutmeg. Grind these along with ginger, garlic, and a little water until a fine paste is formed. NOTE: In the event that green or brown cardamoms, fresh coriander, and fresh ginger root aren't readily available, then the powdered forms may be substituted. In this case, one would use 1 tsp. ginger powder, 1 tsp. coriander, and 2 tsp. cardamom. They would be added at the end with the other ground ingredients into a little water to form a suitable paste.

Heat 4 oz. ghee and brown grated onions. Remove pan from heat, add cayenne pepper, turmeric, crushed green cardamoms, salt and ground paste to browned onions. Then cook on slow heat.

Beat 1/2 pint yogurt lightly and add a little of it at a time to the mixture until half of it is used up. Add fried potatoes and cook for another 5 minutes. Then add remaining yogurt and 1/2 pint hot water. Keep it in oven or cook on slow heat for 20 minutes longer.

Serves 3.

Sweet potatoes and yams are often confused. Yams probably originated in West Africa, whereas sweet potatoes are native New World vegetables.

Yams and sweet potatoes contain simple peptide substances called phytochalatins that are just plain good for you!

CURRIED SWEET POTATOES

8 medium sweet potatoes, peeled and cut into 1" pieces

1 tsp. salt to taste

1 cup loosely packed dried apricots, cut into 1/4" slivers

1/2 cup raisins

1 tbsp. canola oil

1 medium onion, finely chopped

2 tsp. mild curry powder, preferably Madras

freshly ground black pepper to taste

Place sweet potatoes in large pot and add just enough cold water to cover by an inch. Add salt and bring contents to boil over high heat. Reduce heat to medium and cook, uncovered, until tender but not mushy, maybe 10 minutes. Drain well. Meanwhile, in small bowl, combine apricots, raisins, and 1 cup boiling water; let sit until plumped up, for about 10 minutes. In large wide pot, heat oil over medium-high heat. Add onions and cook, stirring often, until softened, for a couple of minutes. Then add curry powder and cook, stirring, until fragrant, for another few minutes. Next add cooked sweet potatoes, apricots, raisins, and fruit-soaking liquid. Season with salt and pepper. Stir gently over medium-low heat until warmed through.

Serves 10.

APRICOT SWEET POTATO

1 baked sweet potato

4 chopped, dried apricot halves

2 tsp. maple syrup

1/2 tsp. lemon juice

1/2 tsp. lime juice

2 tbsp. applesauce

toasted almonds to garnish (optional)

Cut about 1/3 off top of cooked potato. Scoop out pulp. Reserve shell and keep warm. Mix potato pulp with remaining ingredients. Stuff into reserved potato shell. Serve hot.

Serves 2.

White potatoes were first cultivated by South American Incan Indians in the high Andes, and later taken to England in 1586 by Sir Francis Drake. Modern potatoes, such as the russet, are a far cry from the small, flowery originals. Remember potatoes themselves are not fattening—it's the toppings that add inches to your waistline.

As a cultivated plant, spinach originated in or near Persia. It can be either smooth-leafed or, more commonly, of the crinkle-leafed "Savoy" type.

ROSEMARY POTATOES

12 russet potatoes

4 tbsp. extra virgin olive oil

1/4 cup rosemary sprigs

granulated kelp

Peel and wash spuds. Dry well, cut in half lengthwise, and place in roasting pan. (Or you can roast spuds in same pan that you might use to roast beef, lamb or venison.)

Drizzle olive oil over spuds, add rosemary, and sprinkle liberally with kelp. Place in preheated 350°F. oven 1 hour before serving.

Serves 8.

CREAMED SPINACH

approximately 1 1/2 cups raw spinach

1 minced clove of garlic

1/2 tsp. tamari*

2 tbsp. yogurt

1/2 tsp. kelp

1 tsp. lime juice

1 tbsp. grated Parmesan cheese

(*available from some oriental food shops and health food stores)

Wash spinach, remove large stems, and shake excess water from leaves. Reserve stems for making soup stock. Place spinach, along with garlic, kelp, tamari, and lime juice in a large saucepan and steam in the small amount of water that clings to the leaves. When spinach is limp and has turned a deep green, remove from heat. Place spinach, drained if necessary, in blender with yogurt and cheese. Process on low speed until spinach is pureed.

Serves 2.

One recipe that an old Creole lady, skilled in the healing arts, gave to me some years ago in New Orleans, has proven useful in treating those who have no real desire to eat anything and in giving energy and stamina to those who seem to be fatigued for one reason or another. Since Mama Cass originated this remedy, it naturally bears her name.

Louisiana is famous for both its Cajun and Creole cultures and cuisines. This recipe is a specialty of Cajun chef Martin Lafourche, who is a culinary genius when it comes to creating magnificent dishes.

MAMA CASS'S APPLE-PECAN STUFFED SQUASH

2 medium acorn squash
1/2 cup butter
2 cups green apples, finely chopped
1 tsp. cinnamon
1/2 tsp. mace
1/2 tsp. cardamom
2 tsp. lime juice
1 cup pecans, chopped
generous dash nutmeg

Cut squash in half crosswise and remove seeds. Bake with cut side down in shallow pan at 350°F. for 45 minutes. Remove cooked squash from its shells and mix with butter, apple, cinnamon, mace, cardamom, lime juice, and pecans, reserving 1/4 cup pecans for topping. Spoon this mixture into shells and top with nutmeg and remaining pecans. Bake at 350°F. for 10 minutes.

Serves 3–4.

CREOLE SPROUTS

1 tbsp. vegetable oil
1/2 cup chopped onion
1/2 cup diced celery
1 can (1 lb.) stewed tomatoes
1 bay leaf
1/2 tsp. salt
2 cups sprouts (mung, soy, lentil, or pea)

Heat oil in skillet, Add onion and celery, and sauté until golden brown.

Next add tomatoes, bay leaf, and salt, and bring to boil. Simmer uncovered for 12 minutes.

Remove bay leaf. Add sprouts and simmer covered between 5–7 minutes if using tough sprouts.

Serves 4.

WATERCRESS WITH BROWNED ONION

2 tbsp. butter

1 small to medium onion, finely chopped

1 tsp. salt

3 cups watercress, washed (about 4 1/2 oz.)

In small saucepan or skillet, melt butter over low heat and when foam subsides add onion. Sauté for about 20 minutes, stirring frequently until browned. Onions should be dark brown but definitely not burned. Mix in salt and set aside. Place watercress in enough boiling water to cover. Over moderate heat, cook covered for about 15 minutes until tender. Drain thoroughly and chop medium fine. Mix watercress with sauteed onion.

Serves 4.

A CHINESE DISH WITH PRIMROSE

2 tsp. soy sauce

3 tbsp. dry white wine

1 tsp. sesame seed oil

1 tsp. cornstarch

3 tbsp. vegetable oil

1 clove garlic, finely chopped

1 scallion, finely chopped

1 tsp. fermented black beans, finely chopped

1 cup evening primrose roots, scrubbed and cut crosswise into 1/8" rounds

1 small carrot, peeled and cut crosswise into 1/8" rounds

1 stalk celery, scrubbed, stringed and cut crosswise into 1/8" slices

In small bowl combine soy sauce, wine, sesame seed oil, and cornstarch. Then heat a 12" wok or iron skillet over high flame for 45 seconds. Add vegetable oil and heat for another 45 seconds. Drop in garlic, scallion, and black beans and stir-fry for 25 seconds. Add evening primrose, carrot and celery. Stir-fry for 2 1/4 minutes or until vegetables become tender. Recombine cornstarch mixture and add. Stir until thick and transfer to serving platter.

Serves 4.

Watercress is a perennial that thrives in clear, cold water. It is generally cultivated for its leaves, which are used as salad greens or garnishes.

A sensational side dish for summer. Try it!

Your guests will ask for more once they've had a taste of this hearty casserole.

LUSCIOUS-LAYERED VEGETABLE CASSEROLE

1 cup sliced onion

1 cup chopped green pepper

1 cup sliced mushrooms

1/2 lb. sliced potatoes

1 cup thinly sliced carrots

1/3 cup raw brown rice

1 3/4 cups short parboiled asparagus spears ground kelp

3 1/2 cups stewed, mashed tomatoes*

(*You can replace the tomatoes with onion soup and turn this into a different casserole.)

Sauté onion, pepper, and mushrooms in lightly oiled frying pan set on medium heat. Use either olive oil or lecithin from your local health food store to oil pan and baking dish. Next place sliced potatoes in a 2 1/2 qt. baking dish. Then alternate layers of carrots, rice, onion mixture and asparagus. Finally stir kelp into mashed tomatoes and pour over vegetables. Cover and bake in preheated oven at 350°F. for 2 hours.

Serves 8.

VEGETABLE-ARTICHOKE PAELLA

vegetable cooking spray

2/3 cup chopped onion

2/3 cup diced red bell pepper

2 garlic cloves, minced

1 cup frozen artichoke hearts, thawed

1 1/2 cups tightly packed torn fresh spinach

1/2 cup mineral water

2 (10 1/2 oz.) cans low-salt chicken broth

1 1/4 cups uncooked jasmine rice

3/4 tsp. salt

1/2 tsp. Hungarian sweet paprika

1/4 tsp. saffron threads

1 cup frozen baby lima beans, thawed

1/3 cup frozen green peas, thawed

Coat a large saucepan with cooking spray, and place over medium-high heat until hot. Add onion, bell pepper, and garlic, and sauté 3 minutes. Add artichokes; sauté 2 minutes. Next add spinach, mineral water, and broth; bring to boil. Stir in rice and next 3 ingredients on list. Cover, reduce heat, and simmer for 15 minutes. Then stir in lima beans and peas; cover and cook an additional 10 minutes or until liquid has been entirely absorbed. Remove from heat; let stand, covered, 5 minutes. Then fluff up with fork.

Serves 6–7.

HOT RICE DISH

2 cups cooked brown rice

1/4 tsp. pepper

1 chopped onion

1/4 cup grapeseed oil

1 tbsp. lemon juice

1 tbsp. oregano

1 tbsp. parsley

a few olives

Add pepper and onion to hot rice. Then blend in oil, lemon juice and oregano; pour over rice. Garnish with parsley and olives.

Serves 2–3.

Annatto has medicinal value, is an ingredient in the spicy sauce served over the Jamaican national dish of achee and salt cod, and can perk up preparation of ordinary white rice.

ANNATTO RICE PILAF

1 1/2 cups long-grain rice	2 1/2 cups chicken stock
4 tbsp. annatto oil	sea salt

Rinse and drain rice. Heat oil in pan. Add rice, stir and cook a couple of minutes, until rice is translucent. Add stock and salt to taste. Bring to boil, then simmer, covered, until liquid is totally absorbed (about 18 minutes). Let stand 12 minutes before fluffing up with the tines of a dinner fork. Delicious with spicy chicken dishes. Serve 4-6.

To make annatto oil, heat 1 cup grapeseed oil in small saucepan. Add 2 oz. annatto seed and cook, stirring, until oil turns a deep orange color (somewhere between 2 and 5 minutes). Timing depends on potency of seeds. Once color is rich and deep, remove pan from stove. Cool, strain, and store oil in a glass decanter in refrigerator; it will keep indefinitely.

BROWN RICE WITH MUSHROOMS AND THYME

1 cup spring or distilled water	1/2 cup chopped onions
2 cups chicken stock	1 1/2 cups fresh, coarsely chopped mushrooms
1/2 tsp. sea salt	2 tbsp. butter
1 1/2 cups brown rice	1/2 tsp. thyme

Bring water, stock, and salt to boil. Add rice slowly and return to boil. Turn down and simmer for 45 minutes. Stir occasionally. While rice is cooking, chop onions and wash and chop mushrooms. Melt butter in large, heavy skillet. Sauté onions and mushrooms. Add cooked rice and mix well. Add thyme.

Add a little bit of kelp and some more sea salt to taste.

Makes 6–8 servings. (Recipe courtesy of *Country Journal*.)

Thyme is produced and collected in most European countries including France, Spain, Portugal, and Greece as well as in the western U.S.

This excellent dish makes a fine match for seafood. Try it!

LUSTY SPANISH RICE WITH ZESTY LEEK-CHIVES SAUCE

for rice:

2 large Spanish onions, sliced very thin

2 cloves minced garlic

1 finely diced leek

1 finely minced shallot bulb

4 tbsp. olive oil

2 cups brown rice

1 cup chopped, shelled, unsalted walnuts

4 1/2 cups boiling water

2 sweet green bell peppers, sliced with center seed cores finely diced

2 tsp. turmeric

3 tbsp. freshly chopped parsley

for sauce:

4 cups peeled and diced Pontiac (red) potatoes

3 1/2 cups thinly sliced leeks

1/2 cup finely chopped chives

1/2 cup finely chopped green onion

3 1/4 cups water

1 tbsp. kelp

1/2 cup half-and-half

some sour cream

some chopped parsley

Sauté onions, garlic, leek, and shallot in olive oil until brown. Then add rice and chopped walnuts. Stir well and cook until all oil is absorbed. Next add water, bringing to a boil. Cover and reduce heat to medium, cooking until all liquid has been absorbed. In the meantime, sauté peppers and their diced centers. Remove rice from pan, adding turmeric, parsley and peppers. Serve while still hot. This makes a tasty dish when topped with sauce below.

Simmer potatoes, leeks, chives, green onion, water, and kelp in large heavy saucepan for 45 minutes, or until contents are tender. Mash vegetables with fork or potato masher and then puree in blender. Return to pan and reheat a bit. Then remove from stove and stir in half-and-half, sour cream, and parsley. Should be consistency of gravy. Use as sauce to pour over helpings of Spanish rice.

Serves 6.

A low-fat, low-carbohydrate dish that is very satisfying to the senses.

JASMINE RICE AND GREEN BEAN ALMANDINE

Vegetable cooking spray
1/4 cup minced fresh onions
1 cup (1/2") sliced fresh green beans
1/4 cup water

2 (10 1/2 oz.) cans low-sodium chicken broth
1 1/4 cups uncooked jasmine rice
1/4 tsp. salt
3 tbsp. sliced almonds, toasted

Coat a saucepan with cooking spray; place over medium-high heat until hot. Add onion; sauté 3 minutes or until tender. Add beans; sauté 2 minutes. Add water and broth; bring to boil. Stir in rice and salt; Cover, reduce heat, and simmer 40 minutes or until liquid is absorbed. Remove from heat; let stand, covered, 10 minutes. Stir in almonds.
    Serves 4.

Here's a dish that should really bring out the Nature lover in you with its unique "wilderness" appeal.

WILD RICE DELIGHT

1 cup uncooked wild rice
1 tbsp. olive oil
1/2 cup chopped Bermuda onion
1/4 cup chopped green onion
1/2 cup chopped green bell pepper (including seed center)

2 cups sliced zucchini
3 small tomatoes, cut into eighths
1 crushed garlic clove
juice from 1/2 lemon and 1/2 lime
2 1/2 cups boiling chicken broth

Sauté rice in oil until golden brown, over low heat, about 7 minutes. Spread in a greased, shallow 2 1/2 qt. casserole pan. Layer onions, green pepper, zucchini, and tomatoes over rice. Add garlic and citrus juices to broth. Pour over vegetables. Cover, and bake at 350°F. for 1 hour or until liquid is absorbed and all vegetables are tender.
    Serves 4.

POLENTA WITH HAZELNUTS

2 (8 oz.) cans tomato sauce

1/2 tsp. ground cinnamon

1/2 tsp. ground cardamom

1/2 cup pitted prunes, packed, coarsely chopped

1 clove garlic, minced

2 tbsp. Kyolic liquid aged garlic extract (available from health-food stores or nutrition centers)

2 tbsp. fresh parsley, chopped

1/2 cup hazelnuts

1 cup cornmeal

3 1/4 cups water

1/2 tsp. granulated kelp

1/4 tsp. ground nutmeg

1/8 tsp. ground cloves

2 tbsp. unsalted butter

2 large fresh eggs, cracked and beaten

This unique blend of ingredients was inspired by the farcement, a potato pudding with many possible garnishes, including a variety of dried fruits, from the Savoie area of France. Be sure to make the tomato sauce and roast the hazelnuts ahead of time to cut down preparation time.

Preheat oven to 350°F. Place tomato sauce in pan and add cinnamon, cardamom, prunes, both kinds of garlic, and parsley. Simmer on medium-low heat for 10 minutes and set aside.

Next, spread hazelnuts in a square cake pan and roast in oven for 20 minutes or until aromatic and lightly golden. Watch them carefully so as not to overcook. Pour them into clean cotton-cloth hand towel and wrap up. Rub nuts together through this towel to remove their skins for disposal. Then chop nuts and set them aside. Increase oven temperature to 400°F.

Bring water to boil in heavy medium saucepan. Slowly whisk in cornmeal until smooth. Whisk in kelp, nutmeg and cloves. Reduce heat to medium-low. Continue cooking, stirring frequently, until mixture is very thick, about 15 minutes. Remove from heat; stir in butter until melted. Cool slightly.

Lightly oil a 9" square baking dish. Add beaten eggs to polenta, mixing constantly until they are incorporated. Add seasoning to taste and spread half of polenta over bottom of baking dish. Spread half the tomato-prune sauce over polenta in an even layer; sprinkle with half the hazelnuts. Spread remaining polenta over sauce; top with remaining sauce and with hazelnuts. Bake about 30 minutes. When cooked, remove it from oven and let it stand for about 10 minutes before serving. Cut into squares and serve.

Serves 6.

Tofu resembles a soft cheese and is a cus-
tardlike food made from soybeans in much the same
way that cottage cheese is made from milk. It's
quite mild tasting, and has been called "the food
of 10,000 flavors" because it tends to borrow the
flavor of the foods, sauces, and marinades it's
prepared with. Tofu is now widely available in
most supermarkets, having been popularized by the
Japanese.

HOMEMADE TOFU

3 cups organic yellow soybeans
6 qts. spring water
4 1/2 tsp. natural nigari

Soak beans overnight, strain and grind in electric blender. Place ground beans in pot with 6 qts. water and bring to boil. Reduce flame to low and simmer for 5 minutes, stirring constantly to avoid burning. Sprinkle cold water on beans to stop bubbling. Gently boil again and sprinkle with cold water. Repeat a third time. Place a cotton cloth or several layers of cheesecloth in strainer and pour this liquid into bowl. This is soy milk. Fold corners of cloth to form sack or place cloth in strainer and squeeze out remaining liquid. Pulp in sack is called okara and may be saved for other recipes. In blender, grind nigari, a special salt made from sea water and available in many natural or health food stores nationwide.

Sprinkle powdered nigari over soy milk in bowl. With a wooden spoon, carefully make a large, X-shaped cut with two deep strokes in this mixture and allow to sit 10–15 minutes. During this time it will begin to curdle. Next you need a wooden or stainless steel tofu box (available in many natural food stores) or a bamboo steamer. Line box or steamer with cheesecloth and gently spoon in soy milk. Cover top with layer of cheesecloth and place lid on top of box or steamer so it rests on cheesecloth and curdling tofu. Place brick or weight on lid and let stand for an hour or until tofu cake is formed. Then gently place tofu in dish of cold water for 1/2 hr. to solidify. Keep tofu covered in water and refrigerate until used. It will stay fresh for several days in refrigerator; however, it's best to change water daily.

Serves 2–4.

WHOLE WHEAT NOODLES AND SPAGHETTI

1 1/2 cups whole wheat flour
1/4 tsp. sea salt

1 cup plain yogurt

Mix flour and salt. Add enough yogurt to make stiff dough. Knead dough for about 3 minutes. Heavily flour countertop. Press dough out with hands. Sprinkle more flour on top of dough and roll out with floured rolling pin. *It is absolutely essential that dough be very thin!* Let rest 5 minutes. Cut with a very sharp knife into 1/4" slices for noodles and 1/8" slices for spaghetti. Spread on wax paper and let dry until hard, about 3 hours. Cook by dropping noodles in boiling water or bouillon. Cook 10-15 minutes. *NOTE:* These noodles make incredible chicken or turkey noodle soup!

Serves 6.

BREADS & CEREALS

This recipe is a composite of several different recipes from the isles of Corsica and Sardinia and the Roman Empire some 1800 years ago. It's probably the best bread you have ever eaten!

ALL-GRAINS BRAIDED LOAVES

2 cups whole wheat flour

1/2 cup rye flour

1/2 cup buckwheat flour

1/2 cup millet

1/2 cup rolled oats

1/4 cup cooked and dried split peas

1/4 cup cooked and dried navy beans

1/2 cup cornmeal

3 1/2 packages active dry yeast

In a mixing bowl combine *only* 1/2 cup whole wheat flour together with other dry ingredients.

5 cups canned goat's milk

2 tbsp. molasses

2 tbsp. maple syrup

2 tbsp. dark honey

6 tbsp. butter

2 tsp. salt

In a pan heat everything until lukewarm (115°–120°F.), stirring constantly. Add to the dry ingredients above. Beat at low speed with an electric mixer for 1 1/2 minutes, scraping bowl frequently. Then switch to high speed and beat an additional three minutes.

1 1/2 cups chopped wheat berry

1 1/2 cups brown rice sprouts

2 tbsp. toasted wheat germ

2 tbsp. each of bulghur and pot barley that's been previously cooked and allowed to cool.

Using a ladle, stir in the wheat berry, sprouts, wheat germ, bulghur and barley, and as much remaining whole wheat flour as you can. Turn out onto lightly floured surface. Knead in enough of the remaining whole wheat flour to make a moderately stiff dough that's smooth and elastic (6 to 8 minutes total kneading time).

Next, grease the inside of an electric slow cooker, turn the heat on low, and let the pot warm. Then unplug it and put your dough inside, covering the top. Turn once. Let rise until double in size (between 45 minutes and an hour). Really works like a charm and is a virtually foolproof way to make sure the dough rises quickly.

Punch the dough down and divide into three separate portions. Cover with a cloth and let rest 10 minutes. Roll each piece into a 10" rope. Braid the strands together, beginning in the middle and working toward each end. Pinch the ends together and tuck the sealed portion under the braid. Then place into oiled 8" × 4" × 2" loaf pans. (Grease them with olive oil or liquid lecithin from any health food store.) Cover and let them rise into braided beauties until nearly double. Make sure they are set in a warm enough place to nicely rise.

Bake them in a 375°F. oven for half an hour. Cover each loaf with aluminum foil the last 15 minutes, if necessary, to prevent overbrowning. Remove from their pans to wire rack. Brush tops lightly with melted butter to which has been added a tad of mace and cardamom. Allow to cool before eating.

Makes three incredible-tasting loaves!

Dates are sugary fruits that have been a boon to desert dwellers for thousands of years. Arabs claim that there are as many uses for dates as there are days in the year.

INCREDIBLE DATE/FIG-NUT BREAD

1/4 cup warm water

1 tbsp. granular yeast

1 cup warm goat's milk (canned)

1 tbsp. blackstrap molasses

1 tsp. sea salt

1/2 tsp. ground cinnamon

1/2 tsp. ground cardamom

2 tbsp. olive oil

1/2 cup whole wheat flour

2 1/2 cups white flour

1/4 cup pitted, chopped dates

1/4 cup chopped figs

1/2 cup coarsely chopped pine nuts

Sprinkle yeast over water; let stand 2-3 minutes and stir until dissolved. Add goat's milk, molasses, sea salt, cinnamon, cardamom, and olive oil. Stir in whole wheat flour and 1 cup of white flour. Beat well. Add dates, figs and pine nuts and enough additional white flour to make a dough that will clean the sides of the bowl and can be gathered into a ball. Turn out onto a lightly floured board and knead 10 minutes. Cover dough with a cloth and let rest 20 minutes; punch dough down and divide in half. Form into 2 loaves and place in greased 7 3/8 × 3 5/8 × 2 1/4 loaf pans (or pans close to these dimensions). Cover with a cloth and let rise in warm place until double in bulk or until dough reaches top of pan. Bake in a preheated 375°F. oven for about 30 minutes or until bread sounds hollow when tapped. Brush with oil and remove to a rack to cool.

Makes 2 loaves.

(This recipe modified from Eileen Gaten's *Biblical Garden Cookery*, courtesy of the publisher.)

☞ RYE BREAD

2 packages active dry yeast

1/2 cup warm water (115°-125° F.)

1 tbsp. honey

1 1/2 cups dark malt beer

2 tbsp. butter

1 tbsp. salt

1/4 cup plain yogurt

2 1/2 cups dark rye flour

cup pumpernickel flour (or 1/2 cup rye and 1/2 cup whole wheat)

1 cup gluten flour

1 cup all-purpose white flour

1 tbsp. egg white mixed with 1 tbsp. water

cornmeal

In a large bowl dissolve yeast in warm water and stir in honey. Heat beer until warm enough to melt the butter in it; add salt and yogurt. Cool to lukewarm; then mix with yeast liquid. Add all the flours, except for about 1/2 cup of the white. Mix well, then turn out on a floured surface and knead, adding the reserved flour as necessary, for 5-10 minutes.

When dough is smooth, although it may still be slightly sticky, put it in a buttered bowl, turn it once, cover it, put it in an 85° place (inside a cool oven with a pan of steaming water underneath works well) and let it rise until double in size (about 2 1/2 hours). Shape into 2 oval or round loaves and place on a baking sheet sprinkled with cornmeal. Let rise again, lightly covered, until double in size, about 1 1/2 hours. Preheat oven to 375°F; bake for 45-50 minutes. It will sound hollow if hit with a knuckle. Cool on a rack.

Makes 2 loaves.

☞ *Never underestimate the healing power of the aroma of freshly baked bread!*

I love to make big, thick sandwiches using this health-giving bread. Try it!

WHEAT-FREE RYE BREAD

Dry ingredients:

1 cup rye flour	*1 tbsp. olive oil*
1/2 cup soy flour	*1 tbsp. blackstrap molasses*
1 1/2 cups rice flour	*1 tbsp. honey*
2 tbsp. aluminum-free baking powder	*1 tsp. sea salt*

Mix dry ingredients together thoroughly. Mix last four ingredients with flour mixture until well combined; then scrape the thick batter into a well-oiled loaf pan (8 1/2 inches × 4 1/2 inches). Make a dome out of aluminum foil and cover the pan with it, but leave sufficient room for the bread to rise in it. Bake about 70 minutes, covered, in an oven preheated to 350°. Cool on a rack, out of the pan.

Makes 24 slices.

HEINERMAN'S OWN SPROUTED BREAD

I've come up with my own sprouted bread that is an amalgamation of several other bread recipes given to me in the past, with some modifications along the way to improve both texture and flavor. Not only is it different, but you can't seem to get enough of it once you've become acquainted with its flavor. It is a hunger-satisfier, that is low in fat. It contains no preservatives, bleaches, or crystalline-synthetic vitamins.

1 medium yam with skin

3 1/2 cups warm water

2 cakes yeast (or 2 envelopes dry)

1/2 tbsp. blackstrap molasses

2 tsp. salt

1 tsp. powdered cardamom

3 tbsp. cooking oil

3 cups alfalfa sprouts

5 cups flour (1/2 white and 1/2 whole wheat)

Dice yam and cook in 3 cups water until tender. Blend yam and water in a Vita-Mix machine or equivalent food machine until smooth. Dissolve yeast in 1/2 cup warm water in a large mixing bowl. Add blackstrap molasses, salt, cardamom, cooking oil, and yam liquid. Mix thoroughly. Add towel-dried sprouts and about 5 cups of flour. Knead well with fists and knuckles. Place in an oiled bowl, cover, and let rise in a warm place until double in bulk. Punch the dough down and form into two loaves. Place in 2 oiled 9" × 5" pans and let rise again until double in bulk. Bake in 350°F. oven for 1 1/2 hours. Remove from pans and cool on wire rack.

Makes 2 wonderful loaves of bread!

Toasting intensifies the flavor of coriander seeds. Toast them in a small skillet over high heat, shaking the pan until the seeds brown slightly. Then crack them between sheets of waxed paper with a rolling pin or a wooden mallet. Not only are these rounds delicious, but they're nutritious as well.

YOGURT AND CORIANDER BREAD ROUNDS

1 tbsp. coriander seeds, toasted and cracked

1 cup warm water

1 tbsp. brown sugar

1 package Fleischmann's dry yeast

1 tbsp. salt

4 1/2 cups unbleached white flour

1 1/4 cups nonfat yogurt warmed to room temperature

In a small bowl, combine water, sugar and yeast. Set aside until foamy for about 12 minutes. In an electric mixer fitted with a dough hook, combine the yeast mixture, 1 cup yogurt and salt. With the machine at medium speed, add flour and knead until smooth and elastic, for about 10 minutes. *NOTE:* A Vita-Mix whole food machine can be used in place of the other, if a dough hook isn't readily available. Alternately, mix ingredients in a large bowl, then transfer to a floured surface and knead by hand for 10 minutes.

Coat a large bowl with oil. Transfer the dough to this bowl, cover with plastic wrap or a dish towel, and let it rise in a warm corner for about 45 minutes. Punch the dough back down with your fists and divide it into 16 equal pieces. Knead each piece by hand to form a roll and place on 2 lightly oiled baking sheets. Cover with plastic wrap or dish towels and let rise until doubled in size for about 20 minutes. Preheat your oven to 450°F. With the palm of your hand, flatten each ball to form a 4-inch round. Let rise 5 minutes. Spread a scant teaspoon of yogurt in the center of each and sprinkle with coriander. Bake for about 12 minutes, until golden.

Makes 16 individual loaves.

To start your morning off right, bake a batch of these tasty rolls and share them with friends or family.

POPPY SEED ROLLS

2 tbsp. active dry yeast

1/2 cup lukewarm water

6 tbsp. honey

2 1/2 cups lukewarm buttermilk

1 tbsp. tamari*

1 1/2 cups wheat germ

6 1/2 cups whole wheat flour

6 tbsp. sesame seed or safflower oil

Some poppy seeds

*an Oriental-style sauce available in some Oriental food shops and health food stores.

Dissolve yeast in water in a large bowl, and stir in the honey. When the yeast is bubbly, add the buttermilk, tamari, wheat germ, and 2 cups of the flour. With a hand mixer on high speed, mix the wheat germ, flour, and yeast mixture for five minutes. Add 1/4 cup oil and the remaining wheat flour, 1 cup at a time, stirring after each addition. When the dough holds together, turn it out onto a floured surface and knead until smooth, adding only enough flour to keep the dough from sticking. Oil a large bowl or kettle, and turn the ball of dough around in the oil until it's coated. Cover the container and allow the dough to rest in a warm place until doubled in bulk. Punch the dough down until it collapses, form again into a ball and cover, returning to a warm place. When the dough has doubled a second time, punch the air out again and turn the dough onto a floured surface.

Make small balls of dough, about 2" in diameter, and coat them with a little of the remaining 2 tbsp. of oil. Place the balls (12 should do) in the bottom of a lightly oiled, 8" round cake pan. Sprinkle generously with poppy seeds and set aside to rise. When the rolls have risen almost double in bulk, place them in a preheated 400°F. oven. After 15 minutes, turn the oven down to 350°F. and bake the rolls about 20 minutes longer, until they are browned and baked through. Remove from oven and turn out on a cooling rack. Rolls will break apart easily for serving.

Makes 1 dozen rolls.

Especially designed for those with allergies to yeast, milk, eggs, butter or sugar.

AMARANTH BREAD

3/4 cup warm nut milk (recipe follows)

3/4 tsp. non-acidic vitamin C crystals

2 3/4 cups amaranth flour, divided

3/4 cup tapioca starch

1/2 tsp. sea salt

1 tbsp. ground anise or fennel seeds

1/3 cup extra virgin olive oil

2 tbsp. hot distilled water

2 tsp. Arm & Hammer baking soda

Preheat oven to 400°F. Combine nut milk and vitamin C crystals; stir and let stand to dissolve. In a large mixing bowl, combine 2 1/4 cups of amaranth flour with starch, sea salt and ground seeds; whisk together gently.

Next add liquid with dissolved crystals and olive oil to flour mixture. Mix batter with wooden spoon. Sprinkle a little of remaining half-cup of flour in a circle centered on a baking sheet. Put the rest of the flour on a piece of wax paper.

Dissolve baking soda in boiling water; add to dough and stir.

Dough will be very stiff. When water disappears, punch it hard for 10 strokes.

Turn dough onto wax paper. Roll dough to coat it with more amaranth flour. Working rapidly, knead for almost 4 minutes. By now the dough will have absorbed enough flour to be more resilient, yet remain soft.

Now gather dough into a smooth ball, and put it on wax paper. Pat into an 8-inch round, 1-inch thick at edges and mounded slightly in center. To keep wax paper from sliding around, tape it to counter or table top. A floured bread board can be used in place of this, but the wax paper makes less mess to clean up afterwards.

With sharp paring knife slash a deep X in top of dough and place on cookie sheet. Put immediately into oven and lower temperature to 325°F. Bake about 1 hour 10 minutes. Cut inside loaf for a peek: if uncooked, dough will appear darker in color; if done, it will be lighter in appearance.

Note: Needs to be consumed in 24 hours or less because it does not keep well in refrigerator.

NUT MILK FOR AMARANTH BREAD

About 1/2 cup of either raw almonds, Brazil nuts, or cashews

1 cup distilled water

1/2 tsp. pure vanilla flavoring

1/2 tsp. pure maple syrup

1 tbsp. green seedless grapes

Grind nuts to a fine meal in a food blender. Use blade recommended for grinding wheat into flour. Then add everything else and blend for 1 1/2 minutes. Stop several times to scrape down container sides with rubber spatula. Add to bread recipe as previously indicated.

GOLDEN CORNBREAD

1 cup whole wheat flour

1 cup cornmeal

4 tsp. aluminum-free baking powder

2 tbsp. dark honey

1 cup milk

2 egg whites

2 tbsp. olive oil

1/4 tsp. sea salt

Combine flour, cornmeal, baking powder, and honey. Add milk, egg whites, oil, and sea salt. Mix well. Bake in a 9" square pan which has been covered with liquid lecithin (from any health food store), at 425°F. for 25 minutes.

Serves about 12.

A tasty, warm way to start a day.

This is flat out one of my favorites. I once served it to a bunch of visiting students who pleaded for more.

BANANA DATE BREAD

1 1/2 cups all-purpose flour	3/4 cup dark honey
1/2 tsp. baking soda	1/4 cup blackstrap molasses
1/2 tsp. ground cinnamon	1 cup mashed ripe bananas
1/4 tsp. aluminum-free baking powder	1/4 cup olive oil
1/4 tsp. ground nutmeg	1/2 cup chopped, pitted dates
2 egg whites	liquid lecithin (from any health food store)

Sift together all dry ingredients. Next blend well the egg whites, honey, molasses and bananas, add oil and keep stirring. Then turn flour mixture into it. Add the dates. Lightly oil an 8 × 4 × 2" loaf pan with lecithin. Put batter into pan. Bake at 350° F. for 55 minutes. Cool in pan 10 minutes, then remove and cool on a wire rack.

MOHICAN PUMPKIN-SQUASH BREAD

A surviving recipe from the Mohican (also spelled Mohegan) Indians, who were once a powerful North American tribe living in the states of Connecticut and New York and who were immortalized by James Fenimore Cooper in his classic novel, The Last of the Mohicans. *Although they were wiped out as a nation through the cruelty of the white man, several of their unique recipes survive in pioneer journals and diaries kept during that period.*

3/4 cup chopped, peeled banana squash
3/4 cup chopped, peeled pumpkin
1/4 cup olive oil
1 1/2 cups all-purpose flour
1 tsp. ground cinnamon
1/2 tsp. baking soda
1/2 tsp. cardamom

1/4 tsp. ground cloves
2 slightly beaten egg whites
1/2 cup blackstrap molasses
1/4 cup pure maple syrup
1/4 cup brown sugar
1/4 cup chopped, pitted dates
liquid lecithin from health food store

Put squash and pumpkin in large saucepan, with about 2/3" of water. Cook, covered, for about 25 minutes or until sufficiently tender. Then drain. Place squash and pumpkin with olive oil in food blender and mix until smooth and even in consistency. Then stir together the flour, cinnamon, baking soda, cardamom and cloves. In medium mixing bowl stir together egg whites, molasses, maple syrup, sugar, and squash-pumpkin mixture. Then add flour mixture. Next fold in dates. Thoroughly rub insides of an 8" × 4" × 2" loaf pan with liquid lecithin. Transfer batter to this prepared pan. Bake in a 350°F. oven for 50 minutes or until sufficiently done. Remove from pan and cool thoroughly on wire rack.

One loaf generally yields a little over a dozen servings.

Squashes originated in the New World and were introduced to the Conquistadors by Native Americans. They are divided into two basic groups: the quick-growing, tender-skinned "summer" squashes and the larger, slower-growing, hard-shelled "winter" squashes which are usually tastier and more nutritious than the summer varieties.

APPLE-SQUASH BRAN MUFFINS

1 1/2 cups All-Bran cereal

1 1/2 to 1 2/3 cups canned goat's milk

1/3 cup oil

1 large egg

1 1/4 cups all-purpose flour

1/2 cup brown sugar

3 tsp. aluminum-free baking powder

1/2 tsp. salt

1 apple, peeled, cored and diced

1/2 medium acorn squash, peeled, prebaked for 20 minutes and diced

1 1/2 handfuls of raisins

1/2 handful chopped pitted dates

1/2 handful finely chopped walnut meats

1 tsp. ground cinnamon to taste

Beat together cereal, milk, oil and egg with an electric mixer. In a separate bowl mix flour, sugar, baking powder, and salt. Add dry ingredients to bran mixture and stir until well-mixed. Then stir in apple, squash, raisins, dates, walnuts and cinnamon. Pour into greased muffin tins and bake at 400°F. almost half an hour or until muffins have risen and are golden.

Makes a dozen delicious muffins.

Elderberries differ considerably in form and taste, growing from bushy shrubs a few feet high to trees close to 50 feet in height. They prefer rich, moist soil and are commonly found in heavily forested areas, on rocky slopes and in cool ravines.

ELDERBERRY BRAN MUFFINS

1/2 cup whole wheat flour	1/2 cup dried elderberries
1/4 cup cattail flour	1 egg
1 tbsp. baking powder (preferably aluminum-free)	1/2 cup milk
1/2 tsp. salt	2 tbsp. molasses
1 cup bran	1 tbsp. melted butter

Cover elderberries with boiling water and let them soak 3 hours. Sift together first four ingredients. Then add bran and elderberries. Beat the egg and mix with milk, molasses, and butter. Follow this by adding dry ingredients and mix just enough to dampen all dry ingredients, being careful, however, NOT TO OVERMIX.

Fill greased muffin tins 1/2 full and bake at 400°F. for 25 minutes.
Makes a dozen.

Cattail flour adds beautiful color, flavor, nutrition, body and thickening to any soup for which it is used. It also gives appetite to someone who doesn't feel like eating much. The following recipe makes very delicious muffins that are easily digested by those with weak stomachs and poor

CATTAIL MUFFINS

1 cup cattail flour	1 egg, beaten
1 cup whole wheat flour	1/4 cup sunflower oil
2 tsp. aluminum-free baking powder	1/4 cup honey
1/2 tsp. salt	1 1/2 cups milk

Combine dry ingredients first before adding the wet ones. Stir only minimally, probably no more than 15 seconds. Ignore whatever lumps there may be in the batter. Grease or paper muffin tins, then fill two-thirds with batter. Bake for 20 minutes in a preheated 400°F. oven.

Makes about 2 dozen delicious muffins.

The late Maggie Kuhn, who died in 1995 at the age of 89, was one of the founders of the Gray Panthers, an activist senior citizens' organization. In an interview, she revealed to the reporter from the Philadelphia Inquirer that she sometimes took a little cardamom with a few of her meals because it helped to improve the digestion of her food. It has a pleasant, ginger-like flavor, and is valuable for those unable to tolerate gluten. The easiest way to take it with a meal is to put a little bit in a gelatin capsule before the meal, and swallow it with a cup of water.

CARDAMOM COFFEECAKE

1/4 cup chopped walnuts

1 tbsp. each white and brown flour

1 tbsp. white and brown sugar

1 tsp. ground cinnamon

1 tbsp. chilled butter, cut into small bits

1 cup white flour

1/4 cup brown sugar

1/2 tsp. aluminum-free baking powder

1/4 tsp. baking soda

1/4 tsp. powdered cardamom

pinch of salt

1/2 cup plain yogurt

1 1/2 tbsp. melted butter

1 farm egg

some vegetable cooking spray

2 more tbsp. white flour

1 medium pear, peeled, cored, and cut into 1/4-inch wedges

Combine the first four ingredients in bowl; cut in 1 tbsp. butter with pastry blender until mixture resembles coarse meal. Set aside. Next, combine 1 cup flour and the next five ingredients in large bowl; mix together thoroughly. Combine yogurt and next two ingredients; stir well. Add this to flour mixture, stirring just until moistened.

Coat a 9" round cake pan with cooking spray; lightly dust with 2 tsp. flour. Spread batter into prepared pan. Arrange pear wedges on top of batter like wagon-wheel spokes, around edge of pan, overlapping slightly (avoid placing pears over center of batter). Sprinkle walnut mixture evenly over top of coffeecake. Bake at 350°F. for 30-40 minutes.

Serves 4–6.

FRUIT/NUT GRANOLAX

2 cups rolled oats	*1 cup chopped dried apples*
3 cups wheat germ	*1/2 cup shelled cashews*
1/2 cup shredded wheat	*3 cups dry milk*
1/2 cup bran	*1/2 cup sunflower seeds*
1/2 chopped dates	*1/2 cup pumpkin seeds*
1/2 cup raisins	*3/4 cup chopped dried papaya*

Get a good cutting board and either a Chinese vegetable cleaver or a sharp French knife and start chopping and slicing everything up into tidbit portions (the size depends on your own preference). Mix well together by hand with a wooden ladle in a large bowl.

1/2 cup honey	*1 tbsp. pure vanilla*
1/8 cup pure maple syrup	*1 tsp. cinnamon*
1/8 cup blackstrap molasses	*2 tsp. cardamom*

Stir together the honey, maple syrup, molasses, and flavorings. Combine the dry ingredients together with the liquid. Stir until uniformly mixed. Rub a shallow pan with some lecithin (from health food store), then spoon out mixture in an even layer. Bake for 1 1/2 to 2 hours at 225°. Bake a little longer if a dry, crunchy consistency is desired. Have a bowl of this every morning for breakfast and for a midnight snack.

Makes approximately 13 cups.

A very healthy cereal for your family!

SESAME-RICE CEREAL

3/4 cup raw brown rice

1 cup powdered milk

3 1/2 cups water

1 tsp. salt

2 tbsp. whole sesame seeds briefly ground in food blender to make meal

1/2 tbsp. Brewer's yeast

1 tbsp. real vanilla

Toast rice in dry pan over medium heat, stirring until browned. Grind in blender, then toast again briefly in dry pan, stirring constantly. Combine milk powder and water with wire whisk. Put in heavy pan, add salt and boil. Add rice powder, stirring constantly. Lower heat and simmer, covered, about 10 minutes, or until cereal thickens. Toast sesame meal in dry pan over medium heat, stirring constantly for 1 minute or so and add along with yeast to cereal. Stir in sesame meal and yeast. Add vanilla flavor and stir again. Serve with canned or fresh goat's milk and dark honey. Serves about 5.

To really liven up any cooked cereals, just add to them a little pure vanilla, some pure maple syrup, a dash of cardamom, and any fruit you like!

WILDERNESS CEREAL

1/2 cup cracked wheat

1/2 cup wild rice

2 1/2 cups boiling spring or Perrier water

1/4 tsp. cardamom

1/8 tsp. pumpkin pie spice

1/8 tsp. vanilla flavoring

1 tbsp. blackstrap molasses

Combine wheat, rice and water and cook in a covered saucepan for 35 minutes, stirring frequently with a wooden ladle. In the last 10 minutes before the cereals are finished cooking, add 1/4 tsp. cardamom, 1/8 tsp. pumpkin pie spice, 1/8 tsp. pure vanilla flavor, and 1 tbsp. blackstrap molasses for an unforgettable taste! Serve hot with ice-cold canned or fresh goat's milk.

Serves 2–3.

DESSERTS

Bananas are native, in various forms, from India and Burma through the Malay Archipelago to New Guinea, Australia, Samoa, and tropical Africa. They are universally cultivated in tropical regions.

SPICED BANANAS WITH RUM SAUCE

2 small, firm ripe bananas (about 1/2 lb.)
1 tbsp. butter
1 tbsp. brown sugar
2 tbsp. thawed apple juice concentrate
1 tsp. vanilla extract
1/4 tsp. ground cinnamon
1/8 tsp. ground allspice
2 tbsp. dark rum
1 cup vanilla low-fat frozen yogurt

Cut bananas in half crosswise, then lengthwise; set aside. Melt butter in large, nonstick skillet over medium-high heat. Add brown sugar, apple juice concentrate, vanilla, cinnamon, allspice, and bananas and cook for 1 minute. Turn banana pieces over, and cook additional minute. Heat rum in small saucepan. Pour over banana mixture. Arrange 4 banana pieces on each of 2 dessert plates; spoon sauce over banana pieces, and top each serving with 1/2 cup frozen yogurt.
    Serves 2.

Who would ever think that vegetables would serve as a delicious dessert instead of more standard fare like pie and ice cream? Well, in the case of burdock root, you have such a tummy pleaser fit for a king.

BURDOCK ROOTS, HAWAIIAN STYLE

2 tbsp. sweet butter
1/4 cup packed brown sugar
1 tsp. lemon juice
1 cup canned, drained pineapple chunks (save juice)
1/2 cup pineapple syrup drained from chunks
2 tbsp. cornstarch
2 cups burdock roots, cut into rounds and precooked until tender

Melt butter in skillet over low heat, add brown sugar and lemon juice; stir. Mix pineapple syrup with cornstarch, stir well and add to butter and sugar mixture. Stir constantly over low heat until mixture is a thick sauce, about 20 minutes. Add burdock roots and pineapple chunks to sauce and heat through. Serve warm.
    Serves 3.

FRUIT MEDLEY WITH POMEGRANATE SEEDS

2 oranges

1 cup seedless green grapes, halved

2 kiwifruit, peeled and sliced

1 banana, peeled and sliced diagonally

1 cup pomegranate seeds

2 tbsp. orange-flavored liqueur

Peel oranges; cut each one in half lengthwise. Cut each half crosswise into thin slices. Combine orange slices and next 4 ingredients in bowl. Drizzle with orange-flavored liqueur such as Grand Marnier.

Serves 4–5.

NUTMEG-BAKED GOLDENS

8 Golden Delicious apples

1 cup dark honey

2/3 cup water

1/4 cup lemon juice

1/2 tsp. grated lemon peels

1/2 tsp. grated lime peels

1 tsp. nutmeg

1 tsp. mace

Pare and core apples 1/3 way down from top. Place in 13 × 9 × 2-inch baking pan. Combine all remaining ingredients, bring to boil, then pour over and around apples. Bake, uncovered, at 350°F. 50-60 minutes or until apples are tender. Frequently baste with liquid mixture in pan every 10 minutes. Cool in pan. When ready to serve, remove apples to serving dish. Add 1/4 cup boiling water to pan to dilute mixture, or simply use nutmeg syrup in its full strength after heating up on stove. Drizzle mixture over apples before topping with genuine vanilla ice cream. If desired, add rum or your favorite liqueur to softened ice cream and freeze for several hours or until sufficiently firm.

Yield: Makes 8 delicious and invigorating servings.

A brownish-yellow-to-red fruit about the size of an orange, the pomegranate is a thick-skinned, several-celled, many-seeded berry; each seed is surrounded by red, acid pulp.

Particularly appealing during the brisk weather of apple-picking time in the autumn!

Most of the persimmons grown for the U.S. market are an Oriental type—the tomato-shaped, bright-orange fruit known as "kaki."

PERSIMMON-RASPBERRY YOGURT PARFAIT

2 ripe persimmons

1 tbsp. brown sugar

2 cups vanilla-flavored low-fat yogurt

1 cup fresh or frozen raspberries, thawed

1 cup low-fat granola without raisins

Cut each persimmon into 4 wedges; peel each wedge, using fingers or small paring knife. Cut each wedge into 4 wedges, then set aside. Combine brown sugar and yogurt in small bowl; stir until well mixed. Then spoon 1/4 cup of yogurt mixture into each of 4 (8 oz.) dessert glasses; top with 4 persimmon wedges, 2 tbsp. raspberries, and 2 tbsp. granola. Repeat layers, ending with granola. Serve parfaits immediately.

Serves 4.

PRUNES STEEPED IN TEA

1 lb. unpitted prunes

2 tbsp. honey

2 tsp. lemon juice

2 3" strips lemon zest

3 jasmine or black currant tea bags

Place prunes, honey, lemon juice, and lemon zest in medium-sized saucepan. Add 1 cup water and bring mixture to boil. Remove pan from heat, add tea bags and let steep for 3 minutes. Remove tea bags and let prunes stand for a few more minutes.

Serves 4.

Elderberries prefer rich, moist soil and are usually found in heavily forested areas, on rocky slopes, and in cool revines.

ELDERBERRY RICE PUDDING

2 cups white rice, cooked
1 1/2 cups milk
pinch of salt
3 1/2 tbsp. brown sugar
1 tbsp. butter

1 tsp. vanilla
2 eggs
1/2 cup dried elderberries
1/2 tsp. lemon rind, grated
1 tsp. lemon juice

Combine first seven ingredients and blend thoroughly. Then add elderberries, rind and juice, stirring continually. Pour into lightly oiled baking pan. Bake at 325°F. for 1 1/2 hours.
   Serves 3–4.

A variation on a standard summer strawberry dessert.

STRAWBERRIES IN THE SNOW

1/2 qt. strawberries
1 cup yogurt (or whipped cream)
2 tbsp. honey

1 tbsp. finely chopped spearmint leaf
3 tbsp. chopped Brazil and cashew nuts
1 cup shredded coconut

Hull all but the four largest strawberries and chill. Combine honey, yogurt and spearmint and also chill. When cold enough, arrange strawberries and yogurt in alternate layers in 4 sherbet glasses, beginning with spoonful of yogurt. End with yogurt as top layer and sprinkle with nuts and coconut. Place a whole berry on top of each glass.
   Serves 4.

Black, white, and red currants all mani-fest strong antiseptic properties—but, more impor-tant, they add a sensational flavor to desserts.

CURRANT SUMMER PUDDING

1 pint red currants

1 pint loganberries

2/3 - 3/4 cup sugar, depending on sweetness of berries

1/4 cup bottled pure seedless raspberry or strawberry jam

1 tbsp. eau-de-vie de framboise or creme de cassis

1 tsp. fresh lime juice

8 slices firm white sandwich bread, crusts trimmed

1 cup vanilla nonfat yogurt

In large, heavy saucepan, combine currants, loganberries, sugar, and 1 tbsp. water. Bring to simmer, stirring. Simmer over medium-low heat for 2 minutes. Remove from heat, stir in berry jam, liqueur, and lime juice. Let cool a while.

Line 1-qt. souffle dish with plastic wrap, leaving a 4-inch overhang all around. Cut bread slices in half diagonally, then fit them in bottom and sides of bowl, trimming further to fit snugly if needed. (You will have extra slices left over to be used for top.)

Spoon berry mixture into bread-lined bowl; trim bread slices level with top. use remaining bread slices to cover top. Fold plastic wrap over top of pudding, then top with plate slightly smaller than diameter of bowl. Weight plate with heavy can. Refrigerate at least 8 hours or up to 24 hours.

To serve, remove weight and plate, then fold back overlap of plastic wrap. Set a rimmed serving plate over bowl, then invert pudding onto plate. Remove bowl and plastic wrap. Carefully cut wedges with serrated knife and serve each portion with dollop of yogurt.

Serves 6.

A delicious recipe for which I am indebted to Joy Yellowtail Toineeta, a Crow Indian.

A favorite of restaurateur and chef LaMont Burns of California, author of Down Home Southern Cooking *(gratitude to publisher, Doubleday & Co., for its use here)*

HUCKLEBERRY FRUIT BATTER PUDDING

1 1/2 cups huckleberries	1 cup milk
1 1/2 cups white flour	1 egg
3 tsp. aluminum-free baking powder	1/2 cup sugar
1/4 cup shortening	1/2 tsp. salt

Place thick layer of cleaned and drained huckleberries in bottom of greased baking dish. Sift flour and baking powder together. Cream shortening with spoon in bowl, then add sugar, salt, and egg. Stir by hand. Last of all, add milk and flour alternately and continue to stir each time. Pour this batter over fruit and bake in moderate oven at 350°F. for half an hour.

Serves 2–3.

BAKED PAPAYA CUSTARD

4 cups papaya pulp	4 eggs
1 cup shredded coconut meat	4 cups milk
1 orange (pulp, juice, and grated rind)	1 cup sugar

Preheat oven to 350°F. Arrange papaya, coconut, and orange in baking dish. Make custard by beating together eggs, milk, and sugar. Pour over papaya. Bake for one hour. Insert knife in center of custard. If it comes out clean, it is done. If any of milk clings to knife, bake longer.

Serves 4–6.

This is a wonderful dish for children and adults. We often have it on weekends.

SWEET POTATO PUDDING

4 cups mashed cooked sweet potato	1 tsp. ground ginger
1 1/2 cups sugar	1/2 tsp. ground cloves
2 tsp. ground cinnamon	1 cup beaten egg
2 tsp. grated orange rind	2 (12 oz.) cans evaporated skimmed milk
1 tsp. salt	vegetable cooking spray

Combine sweet potato and next 7 ingredients in large bowl; beat at medium speed of mixer until smooth. Add milk and mix well. Pour sweet potato mixture into a 2-qt. casserole coated with some of cooking spray. Bake at 375°F. for an hour or until a knife inserted near center comes out clean. Let pudding cool; cover and chill for a couple of hours.

Serves 10–12.

The commercial tapioca pearls commonly used in puddings come from the long starchy roots of a half-woody shrub that grows anywhere from 3 to 12 feet high.

TAPIOCA PUDDING

1 1/2 cups skim milk	1/2 cup orange juice
1 tbsp. brown sugar	1/2 tsp. pure vanilla
3 tbsp. quick-cooking tapioca	1/2 cup diced orange segments OR
2 egg whites	1/2 cup pitted and quartered dates

Combine milk, sugar and tapioca in saucepan. Let stand 5 minutes. Beat eggs till stiff. Set aside. Bring tapioca mixture to boil over medium heat, stirring constantly. Add orange juice. Cool, stirring occasionally. Add vanilla. Fold in egg whites and diced orange segments or dates. Chill and serve.

Serves about 6.

NOTE: When dates are used, omit sugar and orange segments. Add dates to boiling tapioca mixture before orange juice is added. Cook about 6 minutes. Add orange juice and proceed as above.

A fresh berry delight!

BLACKBERRY ICE CREAM WITH SAUCE

for ice cream:

1 pint fresh blackberries

1/2 cup honey

1/8 tsp. sea salt

1/2 cup milk

1 cup cream, whipped

for sauce:

1 1/2 pints blackberries

2 tbsp. blackberry brandy

2 tbsp. fresh orange juice

3 tbsp. clover honey

Crush berries and combine them with honey. Cook for 5 minutes, then strain through sieve if a smooth mixture is desired. Stir in salt and let cool. Then add milk and fold in whipped cream. Freeze in refrigerator tray, stirring every half-hour when mixture begins to turn to mush. After three stirrings, let freeze another couple of hours. This makes excellent topping for berry pie or tarts, and is equally delicious by itself when served with the following blackberry sauce:

Pick over and reserve 1 cup of smallest and most attractive berries. In a blender, puree remaining 2 cups of berries with brandy, orange juice, and honey. Transfer mixture to sieve set over medium-sized bowl. Press puree through sieve and discard seeds. (This sauce can be made 8 hours ahead and refrigerated, covered, until needed.) Stir remaining berries into sauce just before pouring over blackberry ice cream.

Serves 3–4.

The pomegranate grows wild as a shrub in its native southern Asia and in hot areas of the world.

GRAPEFRUIT SORBET WITH POMEGRANATE SEEDS

1/4 cup sugar	*3 cups grapefruit juice*
1 1/2 cups water	*1 cup pomegranate seeds*

Combine sugar and water in saucepan. Bring to boil over medium heat; cook 5 minutes. Combine sugar mixture and grapefruit juice. Pour this mixture into freezer can of ice cream freezer; freeze according to manufacturer's instructions. Spoon into freezer-safe container; cover and freeze for at least 1 hour. Top each serving with pomegranate seeds.

Serves 8.

Adding a tropical touch to a refreshing summer cooler!

MANGO ICE

1 medium, very ripe mango	*1 egg white and 1 tbsp. sugar*
2 tbsp. sugar	

Peel mango and cut flesh from seed. Cut mango into chunks. In blender combine mango pieces and 2 tbsp. sugar; cover and blend until nearly smooth. Set aside.

In small mixer bowl beat egg white and 1 tbsp. sugar with electric mixer on medium speed until stiff peaks form. Lighten mango mixture by stirring in some of egg white mixture. Fold mango mixture into remaining egg white mixture.

Pour into 8" × 4" × 2" loaf pan. Cover surface with clear plastic wrap. Freeze about 3 hours or until firm. Scoop mixture with small ice cream scoop or mellon baller into dessert dishes.

Serves 4.

A DELICIOUS CHERRY COBBLER

1 cup flour

1 tbsp. pure maple syrup

1 tsp. baking powder

1/4 cup butter

1 slightly beaten egg

1/4 cup canned goat milk

4 cups (fresh or frozen) unsweetened pitted tart red cherries

1/3 cup brown sugar

1/3 cup water

1 tbsp. quick-cooking tapioca

For biscuit topper, stir together flour, maple syrup, and baking powder. Cut in butter until flour mixture resembles coarse crumbs. In small mixing bowl stir together egg and goat's milk. Add milk mixture all at once to flour mixture, stirring just enough to moisten. Then set aside.

For cherry filling, in medium stainless-steel saucepan combine cherries, brown sugar, water, and tapioca. Let stand for 5 minutes, stirring occasionally. Cook and stir until it begins to bubble like a hot spring or small geyser.

Turn hot cherry filling into an 8" × 1 1/2" round baking dish or a 1 1/2 qt. casserole. Immediately spoon biscuit topper on top of cherry filling to form 8 mounds. Bake in a 400°F. oven about 25 minutes or until a wooden toothpick inserted in center of topper comes out clean as a hound's tooth. Serve warm.

Serves about 8.

NOTE: Remember to spoon batter onto *hot* cherry filling. That way, the biscuit topper cooks faster and more uniformly.

For a very special treat try this magnificent dessert which Queen Elizabeth of England and Queen Juliana of the Netherlands have indulged themselves in, in times past.

A CAKE FIT FOR A QUEEN

for cake:

6 oz. semisweet or bittersweet baking chocolate

6 oz. creamery sweet butter

4 large eggs

1/4 cup brown sugar

1/4 cup blackstrap molasses

1/2 cup ground toasted hazelnuts

4 tbsp. sifted flour

1/4 tsp. almond extract

1/4 cup dark honey

1/8 tsp. cream of tartar

pinch sea salt

for chocolate cognac glaze:

4 oz. sweet butter cut into small morsels

6 oz. semisweet or bittersweet baking chocolate cut into tidbits

1 tbsp. blackstrap molasses

1 tsp. pure maple syrup

2–3 tsp. cognac

Preheat oven to 375°F. Grease an 8" × 3" round cake pan with lecithin (purchased from your health food store), then flour bottom and sides. Melt chocolate and butter over low heat in small saucepan placed in a larger pan partly filled with water. Stir occasionally until melted and smooth, then remove from heat.

Meanwhile separate eggs, placing whites in clean dry mixing bowl with salt and cream of tartar. In another bowl whisk yolks with 1/4 cup sugar, 1/4 cup molasses and almond extract, until entire mixture forms a nice ribbon when beater is raised up. Then stir in warm chocolate mixture, nuts, and flour. Set aside for time being.

Next beat egg whites, sea salt and cream of tartar until soft peaks form. Slowly pour in honey, until whites are stiff but not dry. (*NOTE:* 1/8 cup honey and 1/8 cup brown sugar may be necessary to achieve desired stiffness.) Fold about 1/3 of whites thoroughly into chocolate batter to lighten it, then quickly fold in remaining whites. Turn mixture into prepared pan and bake for 45-50 minutes. A toothpick inserted into center of cake should show moist crumbs— not too dry, not too runny—just right! Cool cake in pan, then glaze with chocolate cognac glaze.

To make glaze, place chocolate, butter, molasses, and maple syrup in a small saucepan and warm gently in water bath over low heat. Stir frequently until glaze is silky smooth and completely melted. Be careful, though, that you do not get it too hot. Remove from heat immediately, stir in cognac and set aside until nearly thickened or set up. Refrigerate if you are in a rush.

After glaze is cool, until almost set but still spreadable, you are then ready to apply it to cake. Run knife around edges of completely cooled cake to release it from sides of pan. Cooled cake will have settled in center, laving a high rim around sides. Press this rim firmly with your fingers so it's level with center. Now reverse cake onto a cardboard circle cut exactly to fit cake itself. Place on decorating turntable or on work surface covered with wax paper.

Bottom of cake has now become top instead. Spread sides and top with just enough cooled glaze to smooth out any imperfections, crevices or rough places. This is the "crumb coat," an undercoating to prepare for final smooth glaze. Gently reheat remaining glaze over just barely warm water until it's smooth and pours easily, with a consistency of heavy dairy cream.

Strain lukewarm glaze through very fine strainer to remove any air bubbles or crumbs. Pour all glaze onto center of your cake top. Use metal spatula to coax glaze over edges, coating all sides. Use as few strokes as possible. When cake is coated, lift it off wax paper or decorating turntable and let it dry on rack before moving it to serving platter.

Serve cake as is or decorate with chopped, toasted hazelnuts pressed around sides of cake just before glaze hardens. Or pipe melted chocolate through a paper cone for a more elaborate decoration. To toast hazelnuts or filberts, put them on a cookie sheet in a 375°F. oven for about 20 minutes. Let nuts cool, then rub off the skins between your hands. Then pulverize them, a handful at a time, in blender or food processor, using an on-off quick action to prevent making nut butter out of them.

I love anything made with lavender and this cake is no exception.

WHOLE WHEAT LAVENDER CAKE

2 eggs, separated
1/4 cup hot water
1 tsp real vanilla
3/4 cup brown sugar
1/8 tsp. salt

1 cup whole wheat pastry flour
1 to 1 1/4 tsp. baking powder
(preferably aluminum-free)

3 tbsp. lavender jelly
lavender berries and flowers for garnish

Preheat oven to 325°F. Pan spray an 8"-round cake pan. In large bowl, beat together egg yolks, water and vanilla until nicely thick and pale. Slowly beat in 1/2 cup sugar; set aside.

In medium bowl, beat egg whites until foamy, add salt, and continue beating until they hold soft peaks. Gradually add remaining 1/4 cup sugar and beat until stiff peaks form.

Stir 1/4 cup of the whites into yolk mixture. Spoon remaining whites onto yolk mixture and sift flour and baking powder on top. Carefully fold until blended. Spoon into pan and bake for 25-30 minutes, or until toothpick comes out clean. Invert pan onto rack and let cake cool completely before removing pan.

Spilt cake into layers and sandwich together with lavender jelly. Decorate with lavender berries and flowers.

NOTE: You may wish to serve this cake with warm chamomile tea for a real taste treat.

LAVENDER JELLY

Cheesecloth

4 tbsp. dried lavender flowers

4 tbsp. powdered pectin

3 cups apple juice

2 tbsp. lemon juice

3 cups brown sugar

Line small sieve with double thickness of cheesecloth. Cut a 5"-square of cheesecloth, put lavender flowers in center, and tie up ends to form small bag. In 6-qt. saucepan, combine pectin and apple juice, stirring until pectin is dissolved.

Set pan over high heat and bring to boil, stirring constantly. Stir in lemon juice and sugar and drop in lavender bag. Boil for 2 minutes, stirring constantly. Remove bag. Strain through cheesecloth-lined sieve into sterilized empty baby food jars. (To sterilize jars, immerse them in boiling water for 11 minutes.)

Makes 24 ounces; fills 3 eight-oz. jars.

I love to spread this jelly on toast and English muffins. It makes my day!

Imagine making a pie that requires no baking in the oven and is free of dairy and egg products. For those allergic to such foods, this will come as a real taste treat and surprise!

VEGAN PUMPKIN PIE

1/2 cup dried currants	1 10.5-oz. package extra-firm silken tofu, cut into cubes
1/2 cup dates, chopped	1 cup canned pumpkin
1/4 cup hazelnut liqueur	1/2 tsp. cinnamon
1 cup coconut milk	1/4 tsp. cardamom
1/3 cup brown rice syrup	1/4 tsp. nutmeg
2 tsp. agar	1 (9-inch) deep-dish pastry shell, baked

Combine currants, dates, liqueur, coconut milk, syrup and agar in medium saucepan. Bring to a boil. Reduce heat to low; simmer 10 minutes, stirring frequently. Pour mixture into food processor container; add tofu, pumpkin and spices. Process until mixture is smooth. Pour into prepared pie shell, spreading evenly. Refrigerate until firm, about 30 minutes.

Serves 6–8 hungry people.

A good substitute for chocolate and/or cocoa. There are many advantages to using carob in place of either chocolate or cocoa. First, it has fewer calories than either cocoa or sweet chocolate. Second, it's down-right cheaper. And third, it doesn't have the addictive substance caffeine like the other two have.

CAROB BROWNIES

1/2 cup honey	1/4 tsp. sea salt
1/2 cup safflower oil	1/2 cup granular lecithin
1/2 cup carob powder	1 tsp. almond extract
2 beaten eggs	1/2 cup ground or finely chopped nuts
2 cups whole wheat flour	

Blend honey, oil, and carob powder. Add beaten eggs. Stir in flour and salt. Add lecithin and almond extract, then the nuts. Pour into oiled 8" square pan. Bake at 350°F. for 30 minutes. Cool and cut into 2" squares.

Makes 16 brownies.

Apricots originated in Central Asia. Botanists have characterized this sweet-sour fruit as more of a plum although it does belong to the same family as peaches and almond nuts.

APRICOT RUM BALLS

1 1/2 cups dried apricots	1/4 cup light or dark rum
2/3 cup hazelnuts, toasted	2 tsp. grated orange zest
2/3 cup date sugar	3 oz. bittersweet (not unsweetened) chocolate

In a food processor, combine apricots and hazelnuts; pulse just until finely chopped. Transfer to medium bowl. Stir in date sugar, rum, and orange zest. Roll mixture into 1" balls, arranging them close together in rows on baking sheet; set aside. In top of double boiler over hot, not boiling, water, melt chocolate. Remove top pan from heat and let stand for 1 minute to cool slightly. Dip a table knife into melted chocolate and drizzle it decoratively over tops of candies. (Alternatively, spoon chocolate into plastic sandwich bag and cut a tiny hole in one corner. Pipe chocolate over candies.) Refrigerate until chocolate has set, at least 30 minutes. Rumballs can be stored in airtight plastic container in refrigerator for up to 1 week.

Makes about 2 dozen rum balls.

Because of its mild, pleasant, ginger-like flavor, cardamom can be used in a number of bean dishes, holiday beverages such as eggnog, or baked goodies like Danish sweet rolls, and fruit cakes. It is used in some city hospitals in mainland China in the powdered form and sprinkled on cooked cereal.

Cassia or Chinese cinnamon comes from Burma, while true cinnamon which is light and more delicate is a native of Ceylon.

CARDAMOM COOKIES

3/4 cup white flour
1/2 cup honey
1/2 tsp. powdered cardamom
1/2 tsp. powdered cinnamon
1/4 tsp. baking soda
3 tbsp. melted butter
1 farm egg, lightly beaten
vegetable cooking spray

Combine first five ingredients in medium bowl and stir well. Add melted butter and egg; stir thoroughly. Drop dough by rounded teaspoonfuls 3 inches apart onto baking sheets coated with cooking spray. Bake at 350°F. for 12 minutes. Remove from pans, and let cookies cool completely on wire racks.

Makes 2 dozen cookies.

CINNAMON-MOLASSES COOKIES

1/2 tsp. baking soda
1/2 tsp. sea salt
2 1/4 tsp. ground cinnamon
1 cup (2 sticks) soft butter
1 cup blackstrap molasses
1/4 cup dark honey
1/4 cup brown sugar
2 large eggs
1/2 cup plain yogurt
4 cups sifted all-purpose flour

Blend the first four ingredients together. Gradually add molasses, honey and sugar. Beat in eggs. Stir in yogurt and flour next. Mix all ingredients thoroughly. Drop rounded-teaspoon portions of dough, 2 inches apart, onto cookie sheets covered with lecithin from your local health food store. Bake in preheated hot oven at 400°F. for 12 minutes or until lightly browned around edges. Store in airtight container.

Makes about 48 large cookies.

☞ MARGARITA'S "WAKE-UP" COOKIES

4 dried Chiles de Arbol (a Mexican chile from the state of Guerrero, rated 7 on the heat scale; but jalapeno or serrano chiles can be substituted, if necessary)

1/2 cup milk

1 egg

1/4 cup sunflower seed oil

1/2 cup plain nonfat yogurt

1/2 cup brown sugar

2 tsp. vanilla

1 1/2 cups white flour

1/2 tsp. salt

1/2 tsp. baking soda

1 1/2 cups uncooked oats

1 cup chopped cashews

1/2 cup packed raisins

Be sure to wear rubber gloves when discarding stems from any of these chiles. Then break them into smaller pieces and place in medium-sized pan. Add milk and gently simmer over low heat. Remove from stove top just before milk commences to boil. Let cool and whip in a blender until chiles are thoroughly pulverized. Next add egg, oil, yogurt, brown sugar, and vanilla, and whip another minute. Set aside. Combine flour, salt and baking soda, and stir well. Add wet mixture and stir until well blended. Mix in oats. Add cashews and raisins and continue to stir until oats, nuts and raisins are uniformly blended. Drop by teaspoonfuls onto oiled cookie sheet and bake at 350°F. for about 15 minutes or until cookies are light brown. Cool and store in plastic container with snap-on lid. Take a few with you when driving or working and nibble on them as needed to stay awake.

☞ *Very flavorsome, these cookies do away with the worst form of drowsiness and are ideal to nibble on while driving long distances, operating heavy equipment, or studying for a final exam.*

B E V E R A G E S

A high-protein drink with a wonderful fruity flavor.

FRESH FRUIT SMOOTHIE* FOR FAST RECOVERY

half a banana

1/2 cup strawberries

1/4 cup orange juice

1 1/2 tbsp. of any good protein powder (this can be from soybean or a protein mixture used by some body builders for bulking up)

6 ice cubes

1/2 cup milk (don't use 2%)

Combine everything in food blender and mix for 2 minutes until a smooth consistency is achieved. Variations to this can be made by substituting other frozen fruits for the strawberries, or by substituting 1/2 to 1 cup frozen vanilla yogurt for ice cubes and milk. A little honey or molasses may be added if additional sweetening is desired.

Columbus brought the orange to the West Indies, and it is known that orange trees were well established in Florida before 1565 and were growing in California by 1800. Cranberries were called "crane-berries" originally by the Pilgrims because the flower stamens form a kind of "beak" resembling that of a crane.

ORANGE-CRANBERRY YOGURT DRINK

1/2 orange, peeled, seeded, and cut in half

1/4 cup fresh or frozen cranberries, or whole berry cranberry sauce

2 tbsp. low-fat vanilla yogurt

1/2 cup skim milk

1/2 cup ice cubes

Place all ingredients in in the order given in a blender. Secure the lid and run on high speed for 20 seconds.

Makes 1 3/4 cups of smooth yogurt shake.

*Note: Many of the beverages in this section were tested at the Vita-Mix Corporation in Cleveland, OH for flavor and consistency.

AGELESS GREEN DRINK

Turn back the "aging clock" with a zesty cocktail that is renowned for helping to retain a youthful complexion.

1/2 cup carrots	2 fresh peppermint leaves
1/3 cup celery	1/2 cup spinach leaves
1 large romaine lettuce leaf	3/4 cup canned pineapple juice, chilled
1/2 handful of cut escarole leaves	3/4 cup bottled apple juice, chilled
15 parsley sprigs	1 1/4 cups ice cubes

Place all ingredients in the order given in a blender. Secure the lid in place and run on high speed for 2 minutes.

Makes about 2 cups.

IRON-FORTIFIED GREEN DRINK FOR BOUNDLESS ENERGY

Try this beverage when you experience mid-afternoon slump.

1 cup pineapple juice, chilled	1/4 cup spinach leaves
1 cup papaya juice, chilled (dilute from concentrate, if necessary)	1/4 cup parsley sprigs
	1/4 cup peppermint leaves, cut
1 tsp. lime juice	1/4 cup spring water
1 tsp. lemon juice	1 cup ice cubes
1/4 cup celery stalk, chopped, with leaves intact	

Place all ingredients in the order given in a blender. Secure the lid in place and run on high speed for 2 minutes.

Makes about 2 cups.

*A most nourishing pick-me-up drink,
I make whenever fatigue sets in.*

REVITALIZING TONIC

1/2 cup canned salmon, mackerel, or sardines	2 tbsp. fresh, grated ginger root
1/2 cup canned tomatoes or tomato juice or V-8 juice	1 clove garlic, peeled
	1/4 tsp. powdered cayenne pepper

Place all ingredients in the order given in a blender. Secure the lid in place and run on high speed for 1 1/2 minutes or until everything comes out smooth. Be sure to use tomato juice or a V-8 "chaser" to minimize this drink's overwhelming effects on the senses.

Makes slightly over one cup.

NOTE: For added interest, add 2-3 tbsp. teriyaki sauce, 2 raw oysters, and 1/2 cup ice cubes.

This juice is loaded with Vitamins A and C.

SUPER VEGETABLE JUICE

1/2 cup carrot juice (canned)	1 tbsp. Pines beet juice concentrate powder
1/2 cup spinach juice (canned)	1 tsp. Pines rhubarb juice concentrate powder
1/2 cup V-8 juice (low-sodium and canned)	

Mix everything together in order given in a food blender. Make sure top lid is properly secured in place so that no mess results when unit is turned on. Mix for about 1 1/2 minutes. Drink at least once each day with a meal.

VEGETABLE SURPRISE

1 1/2 cups water, boiling	*1 tbsp. fresh onion*
1/2 cucumber, unpeeled	*juice from half of cut lemon, manually squeezed into container*
1/2 cup tomatoes, fresh or canned	
1/8 cup sauerkraut, canned or homemade	*1/4 tsp. Mrs. Dash*
1/4 cup carrots	*1/2 tsp. Worcestershire sauce*
2 tbsp. liquid Kyolic garlic	*1 tsp. apple cider vinegar*

Place all ingredients in the order given in a blender. Secure the lid in place and run on high speed for 2 1/2 minutes. Makes nearly 2 cups.

This drink combines so many nutrients it probably beats out many popular vitamins.

VICTORY JUICE

2 cups tomato juice, canned or bottled	*2 spinach leaves, washed and cut*
1 cup dandelion greens, washed and cut	*1/2 cup plain yogurt*
1/2 cup dandelion flowers, washed and cut	*1 tsp. extra-virgin olive oil*
1 cup finely cut carrots	*2 red radishes, washed and cut*
1/2 cup finely chopped celery, leaves included	*1 tsp. granulated kelp (seaweed)*
1/2 cup finely cut green bell pepper, seeds included	*1/2 cup ice cubes*

In a pot combine tomato juice, dandelion greens and flowers, carrots, celery, bell pepper, and spinach. Cook over medium heat setting until contents start to bubble a little. Then cover with lid, turn heat down to low, and simmer for 12 minutes. Set aside and let contents cool for 15 minutes.

Then transfer this mixture to food blender of your choice. Add the radishes before securing the lid in place. Set on high speed and run for 2 minutes. Turn off and allow to cool for ten minutes. Then add the yogurt, oil, kelp, and ice cubes. Secure the lid in place and blend for another 1 1/2 minutes. Drink 1 glassful each day with a meal.

Makes a little over 2 glasses.

This delightful juice remedy contains antibiotic herbs that will go a long way toward maintaining your health.

For increased energy, this refreshing beverage cannot be equaled.

VITALITY POWERHOUSE

1 cup canned pineapple, with juice, chilled	1/3 cup celery
1/4 medium apple	1 large romaine lettuce leaf
1/2 small banana	1 large spinach leaf
1 tbsp. English/Persian walnuts	1 tbsp. raisins
1 tbsp. black walnuts	1 small parsley sprig
1/2 cup carrots	1 cup ice cubes

Place all ingredients in the order given in a blender. Secure the lid in place and run on high speed for 20 seconds. Makes 1 3/4 cups of dynamic juice. Serve immediately.

NOTE: Fresh pineapple can be substituted for canned pineapple, but it will create a much thicker drink. If desired, thin with a little canned pineapple juice.

This delicious syrupy drink is a favorite of mine.

SHARON'S DELIGHTFUL FIG SYRUP

1 gallon fresh spring water	1/4 tsp. garlic juice (or use 1 tsp. liquid Kyolic garlic in place of this)
2 cups cut figs (preferably Turkish kind and unsulphured)	Optional: 6 oz. celery juice; 6 oz. pear juice; 16 oz.green cabbage juice*

Boil water. Reduce to simmer. Add figs and soak for 10 minutes. Set aside to cool. Blend water and figs together in a food blender. Then add garlic juice. Take 1 cup daily in between meals.

*Optional juices can be added in place of the garlic for different purposes:

celery juice — for calming nerves
pear juice — for constipation
green cabbage juice — for skin problems

Each of these items should be juiced alone and added separately to fig syrup, but not all combined at once.

ALFALFA TEA

Alfalfa is a perennial herb commonly found on the edges of fields in low valleys. The Arabs refer to it as "The Father of All Food."

5 cups boiling water	*1 tbsp. red clover blossoms*
1 tbsp. alfalfa leaves	*wild honey to sweeten*

After water starts boiling, add both herbs. Stir with spoon, cover pot with lid, and set aside to steep for about 15 minutes. Strain and drink one cup while still quite warm. Add a little honey to improve taste, if necessary.

AMARANTH TEA

Amaranth seed has a pleasant, nutty flavor and plenty of protein. I highly recommend it.

Simply bring 3 cups water to rolling boil. Then add 2 tsp. amaranth seeds, cover and simmer on very low heat for about 5 minutes. Remove from heat and add 1 tsp. of leaves (if available) or else just let steep for 30 minutes.

CHICORY ROOT AND ENDIVE TEA

Chicory is a scruffy, weedy perennial that possesses beautiful, almost iridescent blue flowers. With endive, it makes a fine tea.

To 1 qt. of boiling water, add 3 tbsp. cut chicory root. Reduce heat and simmer for 20 minutes, then remove from heat and add 1/2 cup of finely cut, raw endive. Cover and steep for 45 minutes.

Drink several cups at a time twice a day in between meals, but especially so about 2 hours before retiring for the night.

Brew up a pot of this sensational tea when summer has you in its grip.

COOLING TEA

4 tbsp. cut fresh (or 3 tbsp. dried) peppermint leaves*

1 pt. distilled or spring water

1/4 tsp. real vanilla flavor

pinch of cardamom

1/4 tsp. dark honey or blackstrap molasses

15 drops fluid extract echinacea herb

Bring water to rapid boil in non-aluminum pot. Add mint leaves and stir. (*Oil of peppermint may be substituted if leaves are not readily available. But only add between 6 and 8 drops at most, since it is quite strong.)

Then remove from heat and add vanilla, cardamom powder, and honey or molasses. Stir again and cover with lid to steep about 25 minutes. About halfway through steeping time, add echinacea fluid extract.

Ginger is a perennial herb with an aromatic, knotty rootstock that's thick and fibrous. It's extensively cultivated in the tropics.

HERBAL GINGER TEA

1" piece of ginger root, peeled and chopped

1 1/4 qts. spring or distilled water

juice of two lemons

blackstrap molasses for sweetening to taste

Simmer ginger root in water, covered, over low heat for 25 minutes. Strain, adding more water as needed. Cool slightly for about 10 minutes. Then add lemon juice and molasses. The tea should still be warm enough to dissolve molasses or the molasses may collect on bottom of container.

A variation of an herbal tea remedy often recommended in Japan. It is also a wonderful tonic for skin.

ICED HERBAL ESPRESSO

1 qt. water
1 1/2 tbsp. roasted chicory root
1 1/2 tbsp. burdock root

1 cinnamon stick
2 tsp. green tea, loose and dried

Mix first 3 ingredients together in medium saucepan, cover with lid, and simmer over low heat for 20 minutes. Uncover and add cinnamon stick and green tea. Replace lid and continue simmering for another 7 minutes. Set aside and steep for 20 minutes. Strain, add more water if necessary, and refrigerate. Drink one glass daily with meal.

Loaded with the healing power of nature's herbs, this tea will safeguard your health in all four seasons.

JOHN'S MIRACLE HERB TEA

1 qt. spring or mineral water
1 tsp. fenugreek seed
1 tsp. celery with leaves, finely cut
1 tsp. carrot, with leafy top (if possible), finely cut
1 tsp. red Pontiac potato peeling, grated (organic)

1 tsp. dark-brown vanilla pods, crushed
1 tsp. lemon balm
1 tsp. peppermint leaves
1 tsp. spearmint leaves
1 tsp. catnip

Boil water. Then add next 5 ingredients, from fenugreek seeds to vanilla pods. Cover with lid and simmer on reduced heat for 20 minutes. Then add last 4 mint herbs. Cover again, set aside, and steep for 20 more minutes. *DO NOT STRAIN!* Keep only at room temperature; don't refrigerate. Take three glasses daily between meals. Only then may tea be strained, reheated until warm before administering. Potted tea can be kept in a cool, dry place for no more than 24 hours.

The peppermint plant grows to about 1 yard high and has petioled leaves. An aromatic herb, it has numerous varieties that produce essential oils.

The hearty grains in this tea will have a calming, balancing effect on anyone's constitution.

JOHN'S REFRESHING HERBAL TEA

1 2/3 qts. boiling water
3/4 cup hawthorn berries
1/4 cup grated ginger root

1 cup peppermint leaves
1 tsp. pure vanilla extract
1 tsp. blackstrap molasses

Boil water first. Then add hawthorn berries and ginger root. Cover and reduce heat, simmering for 10 minutes. Then set aside, uncover, and add peppermint leaves. Stir thoroughly, cover again, and let steep for 15 minutes. Uncover and add last 2 ingredients. Cover again and continue steeping for additional 25 minutes. Strain and refrigerate.

A MOST NOURISHING TEA

1/2 cup barley
1/2 cup buckwheat
1/2 cup wheat grains
1 tsp. sesame seed oil

1 gallon (16 cups) spring or distilled water
1 tsp. pure vanilla
1 tbsp. pure maple syrup
pinch of powdered cardamom

In cast-iron skillet, *separately* roast each of three grains on medium heat for 12 minutes, making sure you stir each of them continuously with wooden ladle. The sesame seed oil may be used to lightly grease bottom and sides of frying pan so grains won't stick. As each grain is done, remove it to holding dish.

When all grains have been roasted, combine them in heavy stainless-steel pot and add 1 gallon water. Bring to rapid boil, then reduce heat to lower setting and simmer, covered, for 25 minutes. Remove lid and stir in vanilla and maple syrup. Cover again and steep until mildly warm. Strain and drink cup several times during day. The cardamom may also be added when vanilla and syrup are added, for extra flavor.

THE PAPACY'S WEIGHT-LOSS TEA

7 parts dandelion root and leaves

5 parts burdock root and leaves

17 parts peppermint leaves

15 parts alder buckthorn bark

10 Alexandrian senna leaflets and fruit

9 parts yarrow herb

9 parts witch grass (also known as couch grass, dog grass, quack grass: Agropyron repens)

1 kettle full of water (1 1/2 gallons)

The original manuscript parchment listed these herbs only by "parts" and nothing else. In trying to convert this to something that makes sense for modern applications, I came up with teaspoons —two "parts" of the Latin would be equivalent to 1 level teaspoon of the modern rendering. Also, "a kettle full of water" would be about 1 1/2 gallons.

The page that Fr. Chiaramonti, S.J. translated for my benefit said just to "boil everything until half the liquid remains in the kettle." I took this to mean that *all* the ingredients were added at once, and the kettle was covered over with a lid and simmered on low heat for about an hour or until approximately half the water remained.

STRESS-FREE TEA

4 1/2 cups water

2 tbsp. lemon balm leaves

1 tbsp. peppermint leaves

1 tsp. lemon juice

Boil water. Add herbs, stir thoroughly, and cover with lid. Then set aside and steep for 25 minutes. Strain and stir in lemon juice before refrigerating. Reheat only amount desired and drink lukewarm on an empty stomach several times daily.

Ginger is cultivated extensively in the tropics, especially in Jamaica. The plant reaches a height of 3–4 feet, the leaves growing 6–12 inches long.

This is a nice, thirst-quenching ale that I've recommended highly to those seeking to lose weight. It's a healthier alternative to diet drinks and diet colas.

ATTILA'S SOOTHING BREW

1 lb. fresh ginger, peeled and grated	1 tbsp. cream of tartar
juice and "meat" of 2 limes	4 qts. boiling water
1 cup sugar	2 tsp. active dry yeast

In large wooden (not metal) bowl, combine ginger, lime juice, squished "meat" or fruit flesh, and cream of tartar. Pour boiling water over top and permit to rest overnight. Add yeast in morning and stir well; let stand for 15 minutes. Strain mixture, then add sugar and stir until it is thoroughly dissolved. Store in quart jars.

Makes roughly 4 quarts.

SLENDERIZING NETTLE ALE

4 qts. nettle greens	1/2 tsp. powdered nutmeg
2 gallons water	1/4 tsp. powdered mace
2 thinly sliced lemons	2 cups light brown sugar
3 thinly sliced limes	1 cake active yeast
2 oz. grated fresh ginger root	

Boil first 4 ingredients gently in large open kettle or big pot for 50 minutes. Strain through 4 layers of cheesecloth before adding sugar. Cool to lukewarm. Dissolve yeast in 2 cups of this ale liquid, then stir in remaining ale. Bottle in quart fruit jars or clean gallon jars with narrow spouts. Let stand for 1 week in cool place. Refrigerate 15 hours before drinking.

NOTE: Gratitude to Darcy Williamson, author of *How to Prepare Common Wild Foods,* for this recipe, which has been somewhat adapted to fit needs of this book.

DANDELION WINE

2 qts. dandelion flowers (make sure they're not sprayed)

1/2 gallon water

1 orange

1/2 lemon

1 1/4 lb. brown sugar

1/2 cake yeast

Carefully remove all traces of stems. Place flowers in some kind of crockware. Add sugar, sliced orange, and lemon; then pour boiling water over everything. Let set 2 days, stirring occasionally. On third day, strain into another crock and add yeast. Let ferment 2 weeks in warm place.

RAFFLES' "SINGAPORE SLING"

2 fl. oz. (about 1/4 cup) gin

juice of half a lemon

1 tsp. powdered sugar (honey can be substituted)

1/2 fl. oz. cherry-flavored brandy

enough Canada Dry to nearly fill a 12-oz. glass

enough ice cubes to fill a 12-oz. glass

Pour in all ingredients, except brandy and ice, into capped shaker and shake vigorously by hand for about 20 seconds. Then pour contents into ice-filled glass.

Next, slowly pour brandy over back of a soup spoon so that it lays on top. A few finely diced chunks of fresh pineapple can also be added for decoration.

APPENDIX

LIQUID AND DRY MEASURE EQUIVALENCES

CUSTOMARY	METRIC
1/4 teaspoon	1.25 milliliters
1/2 teaspoon	2.5 milliliters
1 teaspoon	5 milliliters
1 tablespoon	15 milliliters
1 fluid ounce	30 milliliters
1/4 cup	60 milliliters
1/3 cup	80 milliliters
1/2 cup	120 milliliters
1 cup	240 milliliters
1 pint (2 cups)	480 milliliters
1 quart (4 cups; 32 ounces)	960 milliliters (.96 liter)
1 gallon (4 quarts)	3.84 liters
1 ounce (by weight)	28 grams
1/4 pound (4 ounces)	114 grams
1 pound (16 ounces)	454 grams
2.2 pounds	1 kilogram (1,000 grams)

OVEN TEMPERATURE EQUIVALENCES

DESCRIPTION	FAHRENHEIT	CELSIUS
Cool	200	90
Very slow	250	120
Slow	300–325	150–160
Moderately slow	325–350	160–180
Moderate	350–375	180–190
Moderately hot	375–400	190–200
Hot	400–450	200–230
Very hot	450–500	230–260

The following companies have special equipment or food products which can be easily utilized in the preparation of many of the recipes mentioned within the text. This equipment or products will make the recipes more nutritious for you.

VITA-MIX CORPORATION
8615 USHER ROAD
CLEVELAND, OH 44138
1-800-VITAMIX (1-800-848-2649)

America's leading whole food machine (the Vita-Mix) and top-selling stainless steel and waterless cookware (Neova) preserve vital ingredients such as fiber, vitamins and minerals that make consumed foods so nutritious and good for you.

PINES INTERNATIONAL, INC.
P.O. BOX 1107
LAWRENCE, KS 66044
1-800-MY-PINES (1-800-697-4637)

Manufacturer of certain *powdered* vegetable juice concentrates—Mighty Greens, Barley Juice, Wheat Grass Juice, and Organic Beet Root Juice—which can be *added* to many of the recipes contained within the text to greatly enhance their nutritional value.

WAKUNAGA OF AMERICA CO., LTD.
23501 MADERO
MISSION VIEJO, CA 92691-2744
1-800-421-2998

The world's premier nearly odorless, aged garlic extract (Kyolic) is available in *liquid* form to add to those recipes calling for regular garlic, which can boost the body's immune defenses considerably.

TOTAL LIFE INTERNATIONAL, INC.
P.O. BOX 990
MONUMENT, CO 80132
1-800-426-4852

For those allergic to milk, Cool Whey is the perfect milk *substitute* for recipes in this book.

TRACE MINERALS RESEARCH
1990 WEST 3300 SOUTH
OGDEN, UT 84401
1-800-624-7145

In place of salt, which isn't good for you anyhow, try this company's Pure Island Salt Water, harvested from the Great Salt Lake, wherever salt may be called for.

ANTHROPOLOGICAL RESEARCH CENTER
P.O. BOX 11471
SALT LAKE CITY, UT 84147
1-801-521-8824

Rex's Wheat Germ Oil ($65 per metal quart can) is the healthiest choice for oils when cooking or baking.

TED BURKE'S CALORAD SUPPORT GROUP
6002 WEST ACOMA
GLENDALE, AZ 85306
1-800-845-5876 / 602-938-2526 / 602-919-7571

Calorad is the purest form of food source amino acids that the human body needs to thrive on for efficient performance.

INDEX